Masters, 1

COMMENTARY ON THE
MIRROR FOR COMPOUNDING
THE MEDICINE

This book is vol. 1 in the "Masters" series of Golden Elixir Press.

Wang Jie

Commentary on the Mirror for Compounding the Medicine

(Ruyao jing zhujie)

A Fourteenth-Century Work on Taoist Internal Alchemy

translated by
Fabrizio Pregadio

Golden Elixir Press

Golden Elixir Press, Mountain View, CA
www.goldenelixir.com
press@goldenelixir.com

© 2013 Fabrizio Pregadio

ISBN 978-0-9855475-0-9 (pbk)

CONTENTS

INTRODUCTION

Like many other works belonging to different traditions and lineages, the *Ruyao jing* or *Mirror for Compounding the Medicine* presents its readers with a complete, albeit not systematic, overview of the main teachings of Neidan (Internal Alchemy). It does so, here again in common with several other works, in a poetical form, but in an extremely synthetic way. With its 246 characters, the *Mirror* is possibly the shortest Neidan text—even shorter than the famous *Four Hundred Words on the Golden Elixir* (*Jindan sibai zi*), a work also in poetry attributed to Zhang Boduan (987?–1082).

With the *Cantong qi* (Seal of the Unity of the Three), the *Wuzhen pian* (Awakening to Reality), the *Yinfu jing* (Scripture of the Hidden Agreement), and the *Four Hundred Words* itself, the *Mirror* is also one of the texts most frequently quoted in the Neidan literature, either with explicit attribution or by silently borrowing its words, which every Neidan master and practitioner was supposed to have memorized. Some verses of the *Mirror*, in fact, have become almost formulaic: this is especially true of the opening poem ("Precelestial Breath, postcelestial Breath. Those who obtain them always seem to be drunk"), and is even more true of the injunction, "Steal Heaven and Earth, seize creation and transformation," which has been incorporated into innumerable Neidan texts.

Attributed to Cui Xifan, about whom nothing is known except that he may have lived in the early tenth century (ca. 880–940), the *Mirror* has existed in different versions. The version in three-character verses—a particularly difficult prosodic form—translated here is the only one to have survived in its entirety. In addition, there have been versions now extant in fragments: one in five-character verses, one in seven-character verses, and even one in prose. It is unclear which of these versions Cui Xifan (who is often called Cui gong, or Master Cui) may have originally written. The expression *ruyao* in the title of his work literally means "to enter the ingredients"; it is often used in sources related to pharmacology and to Waidan (External Alchemy) to mean that the ingredients are placed in a vessel in order to compound a medicine or an elixir. As for the word "mirror" (*jing* or *jian*), it appears in titles of Chinese texts to indicate that they provide models for the actual application of fundamental principles or ideas.

The *Ruyao jing* has certainly served its purpose of functioning as a "mirror." Despite its renown, however, it also has been surrounded by controversies, due to the reported existence of commentaries that interpreted its poems in terms of what later became known as the "Yin-Yang Branch" (Yinyang pai) of Neidan, which includes sexual conjunction among its practices. While the *Mirror* itself does not contain any reference to this subject, its brevity, its poetical form, and especially its intentionally concise and symbolic language certainly count among the features that made it possible to read the text in terms of such practices, which many other masters firmly and repeatedly condemned as inadequate for true realization.

The present book contains the first complete translation of the *Mirror* and of a commentary dating from the 14th century, entitled *Ruyao jing zhujie* (Commentary and Explications on the *Ruyao jing*), which interprets the text according to the purest Neidan tradition (later called "Pure Cultivation Branch," or Qingxiu pai). The author of the commentary is Wang Jie (?-ca. 1380), also known as Wang Daoyuan and as Hunran zi (Master of the Inchoate). All we know about his life is that the came from an affluent family and was extremely learned, and received teachings on Neidan from an anonymous master in his youth.

The most evident doctrinal affiliation of Wang Jie is with the great Neidan master, Li Daochun (fl. 1288–92), of whom he might be considered a second-generation disciple. Wang Jie edited or published two of Li Daochun's works (which he had received from Li's disciples), and at least one passage of his commentary on the *Mirror* directly derives from Li Daochun's writings.[1] As for Wang Jie's association with the Quanzhen (Complete Reality) monastic lineage of Taoism, which some scholars have suggested as possible, this association is at the very least unclear. It should not be forgotten, nevertheless, that since early times many assertions of connection with Quanzhen do not involve official ordination into the monastic order, and indicate instead transmission of teachings of one of the Quanzhen multiple branches. To give one relevant example, Li Daochun's lineage, which became known as the "Central Branch" (Zhongpai) of Neidan, claimed descent from the early Quanzhen patriarch, Qiu Chuji (1148–1227).

In addition to his involvement in publishing Li Daochun's writings, Wang Jie is also known as the author of two independent works and of several commentaries. The independent works are the *Huanzhen ji* (Returning to Reality: A Collection), which contains essays, poems, and illustrations on Neidan, and was honored by a preface written by the 43rd Celestial Master, Zhang Yuchu (1361–1410); and the *Daoxuan pian* (The Mystery of the Dao), which contains 55 short notes on terms and subjects related to Neidan, or explained in the perspective of Neidan. The commentaries, in addition to the *Mirror*, concern the *Yinfu jing* (Scripture of the Hidden Agreement); the *Qingjing jing* (Scripture of Clarity and Quiescence); the *Qingtian ge* (Song on the Azure Heaven), attributed to Qiu Chuji; and the *Xiaozai huming miao-jing* (Wondrous Scripture on Averting Disaster and Protecting Life), a work that promises salvation to those who recite it, and that Wang Jie interprets according to the principles of Neidan.[2]

In various points of his commentary to the *Mirror*, Wang Jie's prose is extremely synthetic; in particular, he often describes in a few words aspects of the Neidan practice that might require longer explanations. Wang Jie also makes extended use of technical Neidan language, including a few uncommon expressions. This may initially cause perplexities to readers. Having spent some time working on this remarkable text, all I can say about this issue is that the commentary requires slow and attentive reading. Several times, a point made by Wang Jie in his explication of one section becomes clear only after reading his explication of a different section. To understand Wang Jie's Neidan discourse, readers will often need to go back and forth through the pages of this book.

My translation of the *Mirror* with Wang Jie's commentary is based on the edition found in the *Daozang* (Taoist Canon, printed in 1445). I have also consulted the edition included in the *Daozang jiyao* (Essentials of the Taoist Canon, in the 1906 expanded edition), where Wang Jie's commentary is accompanied by those of Li Panlong (Ming dynasty) and Peng Haogu (fl. 1599). I report a few of the main variants in notes to my translation.

This book has been written and published in the context of the project "Fate, Freedom and Prognostication," directed by Professor Michael Lackner at the International Consortium for Research in the Humanities, University Erlangen-Nuremberg. I am grateful to Song Xiaokun for her substantial and constant help in solving issues that I encountered while translating Wang Jie's commentary. While this book could not have been published without her support, responsibility for any remaining error is entirely mine.

Fabrizio Pregadio
Winter 2013

Notes

1. This passage is found in Wang Jie's commentary to sec. 1 of the *Mirror*; see note 3 on page 7. Wang Jie edited Li Daochun's *Santian yisui* (The Mutable Marrow of the Three Heavens), which contains essays and short commentaries on Taoist, Buddhist, and Confucian texts; and published his *Qing'an Yingchan zi yulu* (Recorded Sayings of the Master Who Responds to the Cicadas in the Pure Retreat), which mainly consists of conversations with disciples and of poems.

2. The titles of these works (here cited in slightly abbreviated forms) are: *Yinfu jing jiasong jiezhu* (Commentary on the *Scripture of the Hidden Agreement*, with Additional Poems); *Qingjing miaojing zuantu jiezhu* (Commentary on the Wondrous *Scripture of Clarity and Quiescence*, with Illustrations); *Qingtian ge zhushi* (Explication of the *Song on the Azure Heaven*); and *Xiaozai huming miaojing zhu* (Commentary on the Wondrous *Scripture on Averting Disaster and Protecting Life*).

Translation

Preface

Could the learning of the divine Immortals ever be heard by ordinary and common people? Only those of vast capacity and high ability, only the great persons who possess perseverance and persistence, and only the superior people who are bright and clear could do it.

But then, what do those who follow that learning actually do? Outside, they inquire into the principles of the functioning of Heaven and Earth; within, they understand the mechanism of the operation of their bodies and minds. This is certainly all true. However, if Confucius had not received teachings from Laozi, he could not have sighed, "Like unto a dragon!";[1] and if Gautama (the Buddha) had not been a new incarnation of the saints of old, how could he be capable of seeing that he could transcend the world?

Thus, those who study may be as many as the hair of an ox, but those who attain are as rare as the horn of the unicorn. With no exception, it all depends on whether one does or does not receive the transmission.

The learning of the divine Immortals only consists in cultivating one's Nature (*xing*) and one's Existence (*ming*), and in "returning to the fundament and reverting to the origin."[2] You collect the precelestial One Breath and use it as the Mother of the Elixir, and set in motion the postcelestial Breath in order to practice the Fire Phases. When you use the Fire to refine your Nature, the Spirit of Metal becomes indestructible; when you use it to refine your Existence, the Breath of the Dao is constantly preserved. You entirely change your impure, Yin body and transform it into a body of Pure Yang. The transformations of Spirit are unlimited, and the responses are inexhaustible. Is this not extraordinary?

Today I see many people who study Immortality. When one discusses the true teachings with them, they stick to one or another particular view, which does not accord with the correct transmission of the Way by the masters of the past.

As I look at the eighty-two verses in the *Mirror for Compounding the Medicine* by Master Cui, their words are simple, but their meaning is complete: they encompass the entire essence of all the books on the Elixir. Not being ashamed of my limited views, I have have added notes at the end of each of set of four verses, following the oral teachings of my master. I entirely reveal the mysterious mechanism, and am an eye for humans and deities.[3] In the future, those who have the same commitment as mine should read them and ponder over them with attention. Assuredly, "Spirit will reveal itself, and the Heart will awaken":[4] there can be no doubt about this.

Some, instead, will say that my commentary is not trustworthy. But even then, the words of master Cui should be regarded as truthful. If you rely on them and put them into practice, if you trust them and follow them, you will entirely transform yourself. Then all the possibilities of the learning of the Immortals will be accomplished.

Preface by Hunran zi (Master of the Inchoate)
from Xiujiang [5]

Notes

1. Wang Jie alludes to the famous tale of the meeting between Laozi and Confucius, first told in the *Zhuangzi*, ch. 14 (see Watson, *The Complete Works of Chuang-tzu*, p. 163). After the meeting, Confucius exclaimed: "At last I may say that I have seen a dragon!" As reported in several other texts, he also said: "Birds, I know, can fly. Fish, I know, can swim. Animals, I know, can run. . . . But when it comes to the dragon, I have no means of knowing how it rides the wind and clouds and ascends into heaven. Today I have seen Laozi, and he really is like unto a dragon."

2. *Wuzhen pian*, "Lüshi," poem 9: "I exhort you to probe and grasp the place where one comes to life: return to the fundament, revert to the origin, and you are a Medicine King" (see Pregadio, *Awakening to Reality*, p. 48).

3. The expression *rentian yanmu* means that Wang Jie provides the "Dharma-eye" (*fayan*, i.e., the ability to see the Dharma) to humans and deities, which are the two highest states of reincarnation according to the Buddhist doctrine. At the same time, it is significant that *Rentian yanmu* (An Eye for Humans and Deities) was also the title of a twelfth-century text that summarized the Chan Buddhist history and teaching. By using this expression, therefore, Wang Jie also seems to imply that his commentary provides a synthesis of Neidan.

4. Wang Jie draws this sentence from Yu Yan's (1258–1314) commentary to the *Cantong qi* (*Zhouyi cantong qi fahui*, ch. 9), where it refers to this passage: "On occasion the Numinous Light reveals itself to a man, and his Heart suddenly awakens" (81:11–12; see Pregadio, *The Seal of the Unity of the Three*, p. 119).

5. Hunran zi is Wang Jie's own appellation (*hao*). Xiujiang corresponds to present-day Xiushui, Jiangxi Province.

1

Precelestial Breath,
postcelestial Breath.
Those who obtain them
always seem to be drunk.

The precelestial Breath is the original and initial Ancestral Breath.[1] This Ancestral Breath is in the real center of Heaven and Earth within the human body. [Placed between] the Secret Door and the Gate of Life, hanging in the middle, it is the Heart of Heaven.[2] The self-cultivation of the divine Immortals only consists in collecting the precelestial One Breath and using it as the Mother of the Elixir.

The postcelestial Breath is the Breath that circulates internally: one exhalation, one inhalation, once coming, once going. "Exhaling touches onto the root of Heaven, inhaling touches onto the root of Earth. On exhaling, 'the dragon howls and the clouds rise'; on inhaling, 'the tiger roars and the wind blows.'"[3]

When [the postcelestial Breath] is "unceasing and continuous,"[4] it returns to the Ancestral Breath. The internal and the external inchoately merge, and coalesce to form the Reverted Elixir (*huandan*). Then you become aware of a burning fire in the Cinnabar Field that spreads to the four limbs. You look like a fool or like drunk, but "its beauty lies within."[5] This is why it says, "those who obtain them always seem to be drunk."

This is what the *Daode jing* (Book of the Way and Its Virtue) means when it says:

The Spirit of the Valley never dies:
it is called the Mysterious-Female.
The gate of the Mysterious-Female
is called the root of Heaven and Earth.

Unceasing and continuous,
its operation never wears out.[6]

And this is what the *Book of Changes* (*Yijing*) means when it says
about the Kun ䷁ hexagram:

From the Yellow Center it spreads to the veining, as it
places itself in the correct position. Its beauty lies within,
and extends to the four limbs.[7]

Notes

1. "Precelestial" (*xiantian*) and "postcelestial" (*houtian*) refer to the
states before and after the generation of the cosmos. The precelestial
Breath (*qi*) is the One Breath of the Dao. Once the cosmos is generated,
it is permeated by the postcelestial Breath, which manifests itself in the
multiplicity of the directions of space, the cycles of time, and all the
entities and phenomena that exist and occur within space and time. In
the human being, in particular, the postcelestial Breath is the breath
(*qi*) of ordinary breathing. In any of its forms, however, the postcelestial Breath hides and preserves the precelestial Breath, or one "particle"
of it. In the strict sense of the term, the purpose of Neidan is the
recovery of the precelestial Breath—represented as the Elixir—and its
reconjunction with the postcelestial Breath.

2. The first part of this sentence alludes to the description of the
center of the human body in the *Huangting jing* (Scripture of the
Yellow Court): "Above is the *Hun* Numen, below is the Origin of the
Barrier; on the left is the Minor Yang, on the right is the Great Yin;
behind is the Secret Door, in front is the Gate of Life" ("Inner" version,
poem 2). The Secret Door (*mihu*) is the kidneys, or a point in their
region. The Gate of Life (*shengmen*) is the lower Cinnabar Field, or a
point in its region. — The *Huangting jing*, originally dating from the
second or the third century, is one of the main texts on early Taoist
meditation. It exists in two versions, usually referred to as "Outer" and
"Inner." The "Inner" version" is later and longer compared to the
"Outer" version.

3. This passage is quoted, without attribution, in Xiao Tingzhi's (fl. 1260–64) *Jindan wenda* (Questions and Answers on the Golden Elixir). It is also found in Li Daochun's (fl. 1288–92) *Zhonghe ji* (Anthology of Central Harmony), ch. 4.

4. This expression derives from the passage of the *Daode jing* (Book of the Way and Its Virtue) quoted at the end of the commentary to the present section.

5. This expression derives from the passage of the *Book of Changes* quoted at the end of the commentary to the present section.

6. *Daode jing*, sec. 6.

7. *Book of Changes* (*Yijing*), "Wenyan" (Explanation of the Sentences) on the hexagram Kun ䷁ (see Wilhelm, *I Ching or Book of Changes*, p. 395). The first sentence is also found in the *Cantong qi* (The Seal of the Unity of the Three), sec. 19: "From the Yellow Center it gradually spreads through the veining: moistening and impregnating, it reaches the flesh and the skin" (see Pregadio, *The Seal of the Unity of the Three*, p. 77). In the explication given by Wang Jie, these passages of the *Daode jing* and the *Book of Changes* refer to the precelestial Breath.

2

The Sun conjoins,
the Moon conjoins.
Inquire into *wu* and *ji*,
establish *geng* and *jia*.

The Sun and the Moon are the Great Yang and the Great Yin. In Heaven there is the Yellow Path,[1] which measures 365¼ degrees. In their rotation, during one day or one year, the Sun and the Moon move along it. Coming and going, ascending and descending, they alternately enter and exit. Thus day and night are divided, and cold and heat are established.

In the time node of the winter solstice, the initial Yang is born in Fu ䷖; the Sun moves from the North, and the Moon moves from the South. In the time node of the summer solstice, the initial Yin is born in Gou ䷫; the Sun moves from the South, and the Moon moves from the North.[2]

In one day, the Sun moves by 1 degree; once every 30 degrees it meets the Great Yin (i.e., the Moon). The Moon has no radiance of its own, and borrows the radiance of the Sun. In one day, it moves by slightly more than 12 degrees; in 30 days, its movement completes the degrees of a celestial revolution. Every month, in the night between the last day and the first day, it meets the Great Yang (i.e., the Sun) in the Palace where they both move, and the Sun and the Moon join their disks.[3] The last day of the month is an image of the end of the year, and the first day of the month is an image of the beginning of the year.[4] [The Sun and the Moon] meet and then separate again, separate and then return [together] again.

As the Moon depends on the Sun to receive its light, the Yang *Hun* gradually grows and the Yin *Po* gradually vanishes.[5] In the night of the 8th day, one half of Yang and one half of Yin make the first quarter. In the night of the 15th day, [the Moon] is directly in front of the Sun; it looks towards it, and therefore is full. After fullness culminates, it follows its own principle and becomes lacking. From that day, the Yin *Po* gradually grows and the Yang *Hun* gradually vanishes. In the night of the 23rd day, one half of Yin and one half of Yang make the last quarter. In the night of the 30th day, [the Moon] is black and meets again the Sun.

This is the meaning of "the Sun conjoins, the Moon conjoins" in Heaven.[6]

With regard to the human body, one's own body is a whole Heaven and Earth, and also contains the Sun and the Moon. The body is Qian ☰ and Kun ☷; Kan ☵ and Li ☲ are the ingredients; and the cyclical movements of the Sun and the Moon are the Fire Phases. "The hundred families use this every day, but do not know it";[7] how can they know how to set this in motion?

In one's own body, nothing is different from Heaven and Earth, and from the Sun and the Moon. When you compound the Elixir, you circulate the joint wheels of the Sun and the Moon, and cause Yin and Yang to converge in each breath. When the Sun and the Moon return to the Tripod, Yin and Yang conjoin their essences. When they are heated and refined, they coalesce and form the Embryo of Sainthood (*shengtai*). This is the meaning of "the Sun conjoins, the Moon conjoins" within one's own body.

This is what Liaozhen zi (i.e., Xiao Tingzhi) meant when he said:

> In the Jade Pond constantly squeeze the marrow of Yin
>   and Yang,
> in the Golden Tripod continuously heat the essences of the
>   Sun and the Moon.[8]

After you have understood the joining of the Sun and the Moon, you must inquire into the source of *wu* and *ji*. *Wu* and *ji* are the central Soil.[9] Water and Fire divide themselves between above and below; Wood and Metal arrange themselves in the East and the West. Wood is the mother of Fire, Metal is the mother of Water. Without "the efficacy of *wu* and *ji*,"[10] Water and Fire could not be balanced, and Metal and Wood could not be reunited.

When you operate the transformation, you use the *wu* (Yang) Soil starting from Kan ☵, and advance it by means of the Yang Fire (*yanghuo*); and you use the *ji* (Yin) Soil descending from Li ☲, and withdraw it by means of the Yin Response (*yinfu*).[11] You draw the four images together and let them return to the same furnace. This is "the efficacy of *wu* and *ji*."

After you have inquired into the principle of *wu* and *ji*, you must establish the directions of *geng* and *jia*. *Geng* is the West, Metal, the emotions (*qing*), and the Tiger. *Jia* is the East, Wood, the Nature (*xing*), and the Dragon. This concerns the emotions of the human being, which like to run at a fast pace: as soon as they see something, they chase it and become like a tiger that goes wild. Every time this happens, one's Nature is damaged. When one's Nature is deluded by the emotions, it cannot be the ruler, and becomes like a dragon that soars into the air. Thus the two things become separated from one another.[12]

For one who practices the great cultivation, it is not difficult to have control on this. As soon as it happens, you set to practice. You must rely on the Yellow Dame as a match-maker, and revolve the mechanism of the Dipper's Handle.[13] Within the time of one breath you will be able to reunite Metal and Wood.[14] Nature and emotions will join as one, and Dragon and Tiger will enter the tripod. The Heart will be empty and clear.

This is why it says, "establish *geng* and *jia*." Disciples cannot ignore that the wondrous operation of the Masters of the Elixir accords with the "live *jia*" and the "live *geng*."[15]

Notes

1. *Huangdao*, i.e., the ecliptic.

2. The "initial Yang" and the "initial Yin" are represented by the lower solid and broken lines in Fu ䷗ and Gou ䷫, respectively (the

bottom line is the first line of an hexagram). These are the hexagrams that mark the beginning of the Yang and the Yin phases of any time cycle—especially the year—and of the corresponding Fire Phases (*huohou*) in Neidan. For Neidan, the classical description of the cycle of the year is found in sec. 51 of the *Cantong qi* (see Pregadio, *The Seal of the Unity of the Three*, pp. 97–99).

3. According to the views of traditional Chinese cosmology, this "palace" is found at the center of the cosmos. At the end of each month, the Sun and the Moon move there and conjoin. After the state of stagnation represented by the black Moon, the exchange of the essences of the Sun and the Moon regenerates the Yang principle and gives birth to the next month. (See Pregadio, *The Seal*, pp. 72–73 and 137–38.)

4. This means that in a symbolic way of seeing—which in Neidan is the most important—the cycle of the Sun during the year and the cycle of the Moon during the month are equivalent to one another.

5. In this paragraph, *Hun* denotes the bright, Yang side of the Moon, and *Po* denotes its dark, Yin side.

6. The cycle of the Moon during the month provides another model for the practice of the Fire Phases. For Neidan, the classical description of this cycle is found in sec. 13 and 49 of the *Cantong qi* (see Pregadio, *The Seal*, pp. 74 and 95–97). In the first part of his commentary to this section, therefore, Wang Jie has briefly described the two main cosmological cycles (the year and the month) that serve as models of the Fire Phases. He will mention the third cycle (the day) in his notes on section 16 below.

7. *Book of Changes*, "Xici" (Appended Sayings), A.4 (see Wilhelm, p. 298).

8. These verses are quoted from Xiao Tingzhi's *Jindan da chengji* (A Great Anthology on the Golden Elixir), in *Xiuzhen shishu* (Ten Books on the Cultivation of Reality), ch. 11.

9. The central agent Soil represents the original unity of Yin and Yang. The celestial stems *wu* and *ji* stand for its Yang and its Yin aspects, respectively.

10. This expression derives from the *Cantong qi*, 7:10 (see Pregadio, *The Seal*, p. 72).

11. "Advancing" (*jin*) and "withdrawing" (*tui*) are the two main stages of the Fire Phases, respectively called Yang Fire (*yanghuo*) and

Yin Response (*yinfu*). Through this practice, the four external agents (Water, Fire, Metal, and Wood), here called the "four images" (*sixiang*), return to the state of unity.

12. Here the "two things" (*erwu*) are one's Nature and one's emotions. Wang Jie uses the same term found in the *Wuzhen pian* (Awakening to Reality), "Lüshi," poem 3: "When the two things meet, emotions and nature join one another" (see Pregadio, *Awakening to Reality*, p. 27).

13. See section 3, note 5 below.

14. Metal and Wood represent True Yang and True Yin, respectively.

15. "Live" (*sheng*) means that these emblems are not used with reference to directions of physical space or segments of measurable time, but as images of what space, time, and their subdivisions constitute in the self-manifestation of the Dao.

3

Ascend to the Magpie Bridge,
descend from the Magpie Bridge.
In Heaven it responds to the stars,
on Earth it responds to the tides.[1]

In the human body, the spinal column corresponds to the Milky Way in Heaven. The Milky Way separates [Heaven into two parts], but a divine magpie builds a bridge; this is why we speak of the Magpie Bridge. In the human being, the tongue is called Magpie Bridge.[2]

When you compound the Elixir, you always use the Yellow Dame to lead the Infant to ascend to the Muddy Pellet and conjoin with the Lovely Maid.[3] This is called "ascending to the Magpie Bridge." [Then] the Yellow Dame again goes back and forth; smiling, she leads the Infant and the Lovely Maid to return together to the Cavern Chamber.[4] [To do so], they must come down from the Muddy Pellet; therefore it says, "descend from the Magpie Bridge."

It is not that there are truly a Yellow Dame, an Infant, and a Lovely Maid: this is a speech made through metaphors, and concerns nothing outside the body, the mind, and the Intention (*yi*). Through the efficacy of silent operation, internally you rely on the movement of the Celestial Net, and externally you use the motion of the Dipper's Handle.[5] When you kindle the Fire, you become aware of the Breath ascending without interruption. Similar to the initial rise of a tide, it goes upwards by inverting its flow; therefore it says, "in Heaven it responds to the stars, on Earth it responds to the tides."

This is what a scripture on the Elixir means when it says:

The practice is easy, the Medicine is not far away.[6]

And this is what we mean when we say: "The wheel of Heaven revolves, and the Earth responds with the tides."

Notes

1. For the translation of the first two verses, see the next note.

2. According to a Chinese legend, the Magpie Bridge connects the Altair and Vega stars across the Milky Way, so that the Herdboy and the Weaving Girl, who live in those stars and love one another, can meet once a year. In Neidan, the Magpie Bridge connects the Function and Control vessels (*renmai* and *dumai*), which respectively run along the front and the back of the body and make the conjunction of Yin and Yang possible. According to different views, this Bridge is either the tongue or the nose. In another view, there are an upper Bridge, which is the tongue, and a lower Bridge, which is found at the bottom of the spine. In accordance with the second view, the first two verses of this stanza should be translated as "The upper Magpie Bridge, / the lower Magpie Bridge." In his commentary, Wang Jie mentions only the tongue, and understands *shang* and *xia* ("upper" and "lower") as verbs meaning "to ascend" and "to descend," respectively to and from the Magpie Bridge. To avoid inconsistencies between text and commentary, I have translated this stanza in accordance with Wang Jie's reading.

3. Muddy Pellet (*niwan*) is the most common name of the upper Cinnabar Field, located in the region of the head.

4. Cavern Chamber (*dongfang*) is usually a name of one of the "chambers" of the Muddy Pellet (the upper Cinnabar Field), but here clearly connotes the lower Cinnabar Field. In both Classical and present-day Chinese, this term is also used to mean "nuptial chamber."

5. Celestial Net (*tiangang*) is the name of the first four stars of the Northern Dipper, and Dipper's Handle (*doubing*) is the name of its last three stars. Through its apparent rotation in the sky, the Northern Dipper distributes Breath (*qi*) to the whole cosmos. For this reason, it is also taken as a model for the circulation of Breath within the human body.

6. *Wuzhen pian,* "Xijiang yue," poem 2 (see Cleary, *Understanding Reality,* p. 132).

4

Raise the wind of Xun ☴,
circulate the fire of Kun ☷.
They enter the Yellow Room
and form the perfect Treasure.

The method of compounding the Elixir consists in refining the True Lead and the True Mercury found in one's own body. "When Lead meets the birth of *gui*,"[1] you must activate the wind of Xun ☴ and fan the furnace with the bellows.[2] Circulate the Fire of the Palace of Kun ☷, which is hidden below. Extract the Yang within Kan ☵ to replenish the Yin within Li ☲ and form the image of Qian ☰. Stop when you return to the position of Kun. In the blink of an eye, issue the Fire and refine. When the Lead is clear and the Mercury is pure, they will coalesce and form the Golden Embryo, which is equal to Emptiness and is indestructible for countless eons. This is why it says, "they enter the Yellow Room and form the perfect Treasure."[3]

This is what the *Duren jing* (Scripture on Salvation) means when it says:

Within, it regulates the five Breaths
and inchoately merges the hundred spirits.
In ten cycles, it returns to the Numen,
and the ten thousand Breaths all attain immortality.[4]

And it is what Xiao Tingzhi meant when he said:

The Great Medicines are three — Essence, Breath, and
  Spirit;
the celestial child and mother love one another.

Through the turning of the wind they join inchoately and
  return to the True Body:
the practice of refining renews them every day.[5]

Notes

1. *Wuzhen pian*, "Lüshi," poem 7 (see Pregadio, *Awakening*, p. 42).
The earthly branch *gui* represents the postcelestial aspect of Water, or
Kan ☵. This verse, often quoted in Neidan texts, means that one
should collect Lead, or True Yang, as soon as it is born within Kun ☷.

2. Among natural phenomena, the trigram Xun ☴ stands for the
wind. The expression "wind of Xun" means breath.

3. Yellow Room (*huangfang*) is a synonym of Yellow Court (*huangting*), one of the names of the lower Cinnabar Field.

4. *Lingbao wuliang duren shangpin miaojing* (Wondrous Scripture
of the Upper Chapters of the Numinous Treasure on Limitless Salvation), ch. 1; see Bokenkamp, *Early Daoist Scriptures*, p. 423. The *Duren
jing* is one of the main scriptures in the Lingbao (Numinous Treasure)
corpus, which was created in the early fourth century and is mainly
concerned with Taoist ritual. Several centuries later, this scripture also
attracted the interest of some Neidan masters, who wrote commentaries on it. In the Neidan reading of this passage, the "ten cycles" are
the ten months of gestation of the Embryo.

5. These verses are quoted from Xiao Tingzhi's *Jindan da chengji*,
in *Xiuzhen shishu*, ch. 11. The "wind" is Breath (*qi*).

5

> Water fears dryness,
> Fire fears cold.
> Make an error as fine as a hair,
> and they will not form the Elixir.

The essential in the cultivation of Reality and the internal refining is that the Water in the tripod should not dry, and the Fire in the stove should not cool. A scripture on the Elixir says:

> In the Golden Tripod constantly maintain water and fire warm,
> in the Jade Furnace do not let the fire become cold.[1]

To explain this in terms of the External Elixir (*waidan*), when you compound the Elixir, you always apply the functions of the fierce refining and the gentle heating. The most important thing is harmonizing the force of the fire. If the fire is too strong, it would scorch and the water would dry; if it is not sufficient, the water would be in excess and the fire would cool.[2] The main point lies in maintaining the continuity. In a while (*yike*)[3] [you perform] a whole celestial revolution. When Water and Fire have been balanced, the Elixir coalesces within the Tripod. This happens of itself. But if you "make an error as fine as a hair," then "they will not form the Elixir."

An Immortal Master said:

> Among the medicines there the old and the tender,
> in the Fire there are pounds and ounces.[4]

Disciples cannot ignore this. This is what Liaozhen zi (i.e., Xiao Tingzhi) meant when he said:

> For the seven returns and the nine reversions, you must
>   know what is important;
> in the practice, you must not make an error as fine as a
>   hair.[5]

And this is what the *Wuzhen pian* (Awakening to Reality) means
when it says:

> On the whole, it all depends on the force of practice:
> with an error as fine as a hair, you will not make the
>   Elixir.[6]

Notes

1. Taoist texts attribute these verses to Xue Daoguang (1078?–1191,
third patriarch of the Southern Lineage of Neidan), but they are not
found in his *Huandan fuming pian* (Returning to Life through the
Reverted Elixir).

2. For this sentence, I follow the text in the *Daozang jiyao*. The
Daozang text reads, "If the fire is too strong, it would scorch and the
water would be in excess; if it is not sufficient, the water would dry and
the fire would cool."

3. If the expression *yike* is understood literally, it denotes a time
span corresponding to about 15 minutes. Wang Jie also uses this
expression in his commentary to sections 8, 15, and 16.

4. I have not identified the source of these verses. The terms
"old" (*lao*) and "tender" (or "young," *nen*) are used in the context of
the Fire Phases: an ingredient that has not been submitted to sufficient
heating is said to be still "tender," while one that has received too much
heat is said to be "old."

5. These verses are quoted from Xiao Tingzhi's *Jindan da chengji*,
in *Xiuzhen shishu*, ch. 11.

6. *Wuzhen pian*, "Jueju," poem 27 (see Cleary, *Understanding
Reality*, p. 85).

6

The Lead-Dragon ascends,
the Mercury-Tiger descends.
Force the Two Things,
do not be indulgent.

Lead is the one particle of True Yang within Kan ☵; we call it Dragon. Mercury is the one particle of True Yin within Li ☲; we call it Tiger.

When you compound the Elixir, you always move the *wu* (Yang) Soil upwards to extract the Lead within Kan. Wood generates Fire, which blazes and ascends to the Muddy Pellet. Since the Dragon comes forth from the Fire, it says "the Lead-Dragon ascends." You [also] use the *ji* (Yin) Soil to draw the Mercury within Li. Metal generates Water, which flows and descends to the [lower] Cinnabar Field. Since the Tiger is born in the Water, it says "the Mercury-Tiger descends."

In the practice of seizing [the ingredients], if you do not apply the strength of the fierce Fire, the Lead-Dragon would not ascend; and if you do not use the strength of the gentle Fire, the Mercury-Tiger would not descend. The wonder of the cyclical flow [that occurs] during each breath lies in the amount of force [that you apply]. Use your strength to seize the Dragon and the Tiger, and place them in the Tripod. Heat and refine them, and they will transmute themselves into a royal jelly (*wangjiang*). Therefore it says, "force the Two Things, do not be indulgent."

This is what Zhang Ziyang (i.e., Zhang Boduan) meant when he said:

The White Tiger in the Western Mountain by nature goes
   wild,
the Green Dragon in the Eastern Sea cannot be defied.
Grab each of them in your hands and let them battle to
   death;
refine them, and they will turn into a chunk of purple
   golden frost.[1]

Notes

1. *Wuzhen pian*, "Jueju," poem 20 (see Cleary, *Understanding Reality*, p. 79, where this is poem 21). Zhang Boduan (987?–1082), the author of the *Wuzhen pian*, was placed at the origins of the Southern Lineage (Nanzong) of Neidan, and his work has played a deep influence on the whole history of Internal Alchemy in China.

7

It is born in Kun ☷
and is planted in Qian ☰.
Just be thoroughly sincere,
and model yourself on what is so of its own.

Zhang Ziyang (i.e., Zhang Boduan) said:

> You should know that the source of the stream, the place
> where the Medicine is born,
> is just at the southwest — that is its native village.[1]

This is why it is said that the southwestern direction in one's own
body is the position of Kun ☷. A human being's belly is Kun, and
its head is Qian ☰. Kun dwells below and is the Furnace, Qian
dwells above and is the Tripod. The Great Medicine of the Gold-
en Elixir "is born in Kun and is planted in Qian."

When you collect the ingredients to compound the Elixir, you
must always start from the position of Kun, which lies hidden in
the Caudal Cavity, and "nourish warmly."[2] When you see the
Dragon you should apply a fierce Fire, and force the Breath of True
Yang to invert its course and ascend to the Palace of Qian, where
the conjunction [of Breath and Spirit] occurs.[3] Stop when you
return to the position of Kun. As you heat [the ingredients] with an
extremely intense fire, they coalesce and form the perfect Treasure.
Therefore it says, "it is born in Kun and is planted in Qian."

Within all this, there are also [teachings about] the precelestial
time of the birth of the Medicine, [and about the practices of]
contemplating the Heart (*guanxin*), inhaling the Spirit (*xishen*),
and "grasping without dispersion" (*woding buxie*), which assist
the strength of the Fire Phases. The ancient Immortals constantly
kept [these subjects] secret, and did not talk about them. This is

the highest mechanism: who is able to know it?[4]

The scope of the practice consists only in maintaining sincerity (*cuncheng*).[5] If in "avoiding dangers in the fight in the wild" you model yourself on Heaven and take the Earth as your image, the corresponding transformations occur of their own.[6] Therefore it says, "just be thoroughly sincere, and model yourself on what is so of its own."

Notes

1. *Wuzhen pian*, "Lüshi," poem 7 (see Pregadio, *Awakening*, p. 42).

2. The Caudal Cavity (*weixue*) is found under the first segment of the spinal column.

3. Spirit resides in the upper Cinnabar Field. When Breath reaches the upper Cinnabar Field, it conjoins with Spirit.

4. This passage is partly drawn from Yu Yan's commentary to the *Cantong qi* (*Zhouyi cantong qi fahui*, ch. 4). Concerning the "precelestial time of the birth of the Medicine," Yu Yan implies that it pertains to a different time dimension compared to the time of the Neidan practice.

5. The expression "maintaining sincerity" defines one of the cardinal concepts in Neidan: "sincerity" is equivalent to the True Intention (*zhenyi*), which is the operation of Spirit. This expression derives from the *Book of Changes*, "Wenyan" (Explanation of the Sentences) on the hexagram Qian ☰: "Even in ordinary speech he is trustworthy, and in ordinary actions he is careful. He wards off evil and maintains his sincerity" (see Wilhelm, p. 380).

6. The "fight in the wild" (*yezhan*) is the moment in which Yin and Yang conjoin and give birth to the Yang principle (Fu ䷗), or to the Elixir. This expression derives from *Cantong qi*, 49:37–38: "'Nine at the top, arrogant dragon' / fighting for power in the wild" (see Pregadio, *The Seal*, p. 96). In the *Cantong qi*, this refers to the "fight" that occurs in the night of new moon, when the Yin principle has concluded its cycle and and the Yang principle is ready to rise again. "Nine on top, arrogant dragon" in turn comes from the *Book of Changes*, last line ("nine on top") of the hexagram Qian ☰.

8

Steal Heaven and Earth,
seize creation and transformation.
Gather the five agents,
bring the eight trigrams together.

Clenching Heaven and Earth, grasping Yin and Yang, gathering the five agents, and bringing the eight trigrams together: this is the learning of the divine immortals.

Heaven and Earth are Qian and Kun. Creation and transformation are Yin and Yang. The five agents are Metal, Wood, Water, Fire, and Soil. The eight trigrams are Qian ☰, Kun ☷, Kan ☵, Li ☲, Zhen ☳, Xun ☴, Gen ☶, and Dui ☱.

However, the greatness of Heaven and Earth, and the depth of creation and transformation, lies in the fact that the five agents part and distribute themselves, and that the eight trigrams arrange themselves in a ring. By which art can you steal them and seize them, cause them to gather and bring them together?

"To steal" means to rob; "to seize" means to take; "to gather" means to converge; "to bring together" means to join. This concerns the methods of the Masters of the Elixir, whose wonder lies in the oral transmission. The true instructions on compounding the Elixir always pertain to this and nothing else. Wait until the time comes and the Breath transmutes itself: when the Medicine is produced, the Spirit knows it. Then you must shut the Barrier of Wind, close the Door of Gen ☶, turn the Celestial Net, and revolve the Dipper's Handle.[1] As each breath allows the Matching Fires [of Yin and Yang] to circulate, it causes 3,600 correct Breaths (*zhengqi*) to converge, and inverts the series of the 72 periods.[2]

When you have reversed the five agents and have brought the

eight trigrams together, and all of them have returned to the Earthenware Crucible, close it and firmly seal it.[3] Immediately harmonize the Fire that you send forth, and refine by means of an intense, fierce heat. [The Medicine] will coalesce and form the Embryo of Sainthood.

In this way, by practicing for a while you seize the nodal times of one whole year. A scripture on the Elixir says:

> If the human Heart joins with the Heart of Heaven,
> reversing Yin and Yang takes only one instant.[4]

This means that with one exhalation and one inhalation you can "seize creation and transformation." In one day, a human being makes 13,500 exhalations and 13,500 inhalations. One exhalation and one inhalation correspond to one breath; thus in the space of one breath, you hiddenly seize a celestial revolution of 13,500 years. In one year, you make 4,860,000 breaths, and you hiddenly seize a celestial revolution of 4,860,000 years. At that point, you entirely change your impure Yin body and transform it into a body of Pure Yang.

The transformations of Spirit are unlimited: coagulation results in form, dispersion results in wind.[5] You exit Being and enter Non-Being, and whether you conceal yourself or let yourself be seen, you cannot be fathomed. Is this not extraordinary?

Notes

1. The Barrier of Wind (*fengguan*) is one of the two openings under the palate that allow the passage of air during inhalation and exhalation. — For "door of Gen ☶," the text in the *Daozang jiyao* has "door of Dui ☱." Dui usually represents the mouth.

2. The 3,600 correct Breaths are often said to be those of 3,600 years, but this number also corresponds to the "double hours" contained in the ten months of gestation of the Embryo. The 72 periods are the 5-day phases that form one year.

3. Earthenware Crucible (*tufu*), a name derived from Waidan (Exter-

nal Alchemy), denotes in Neidan the lower Cinnabar Field.

4. These verses are quoted from Xiao Tingzhi's *Jindan da chengji*, in *Xiuzhen shishu*, ch. 9.

5. These sentences are found in many Taoist texts. The last word is usually "breath" (*qi*) instead of "wind" (*feng*), but the two terms are obviously equivalent in this context.

9

Water is True Water,
Fire is True Fire.
Water and Fire conjoin:
you will never grow old.

Water dwells in the North. Among the trigrams it is Kan ☵, and
in the body it is the kidneys. Fire dwells in the South. Among the
trigrams it is Li ☲, and in the body it is the heart. Water stores
Fire within itself, and Fire stores Water within itself. In the human
being, the one particle of True Liquor within the heart is the True
Water, and the one particle of True Yang within the kidneys is the
True Fire.

Water and Fire are divided between above and below. How can
they be conjoined? You must avail yourself of the True Soil of *wu*
and *ji*[1] in order to seize and control the True Fire and the True
Water, and to apply pressure on them. Thus you can cause them
to ascend and descend, and to return together to the Earthenware
Crucible.

After Water and Fire have been balanced, they coalesce and
form the Golden Elixir, which is the Pure Yang of the One Breath
and is as longevous as Heaven. Therefore it says, "Water and Fire
conjoin: you will never grow old."

Notes

1. I.e., the Center.

10

Water can flow,
Fire can burn.
Within oneself,
this can be verified.

Since Water is above, it is able to flow and wet what is below; since Fire is below, it is able to blaze and burn what is above. This is the natural principle of the ascent and descent of Water and Fire in Heaven and Earth. In compounding the Elixir within the human body, you operate in the same way. Therefore it says, "within oneself, this can be verified."

11

It is Nature and Existence,
it is not Spirit and Breath.
Lead in the village of Water:
the one ingredient.

One's Nature (*xing*) is Spirit, one's Existence (*ming*) is Breath. The inchoate merging of Nature and Existence is the precelestial foundation; the cyclical transformations of Spirit and Breath are the postcelestial operation. Therefore it says, "it is Nature and Existence, it is not Spirit and Breath."

If those who devote themselves to self-cultivation want to make their Nature numinous and their Existence firm, from the moment they set to practice they must collect the Lead in the village of Water. "Lead in the village of Water" means that Kun ☷ is breached by Qian ☰ and becomes Kan ☵. [Therefore] within the Kan-Water there is the Qian-Metal:

> Metal is the mother of Water —
> the mother is hidden in the embryo of her son.[1]

One particle of True Yang dwells in it. As soon as you meet the movement of the Yang principle in the *zi* hour within yourself, you should immediately collect it. Ziyang (i.e., Zhang Boduan) said:

> When Lead meets the birth of *gui*, quickly you should
> collect it.[2]

He meant that at the time of the collection you must use the Intention, which goes back and forth, and lead the Fire so that it forces the Metal [to ascend]. This is exactly what is meant by the words:

Fire forces Metal into movement, following an inverted
course,
and the Great Elixir coagulates of its own within the
Tripod.[3]

This one ingredient is the root of the Great Dao.
Yunfang (i.e., Zhongli Quan) said:

The Gate that gives me life is the Door that gives me
death:
how many people are aware of this, how many are awak-
ened to it?
When the night comes, even the strongest of all men pon-
ders meticulously:
living a long life without dying depends on each of us.[4]

He pointed to this one ingredient because he wished the people of
this world to seek it in this way, as it is the foundation for refining
the Elixir. This is what the scriptures on the Elixir mean when
they say:

Hold True Lead firmly and seek with intention[5]

and when they say:

Just take the one ingredient, the Metal within Water.[6]

Notes

1. *Cantong qi*, 23:1–2 (see Pregadio, *The Seal*, p. 79). This is one of
the sentences most frequently quoted in Neidan texts. It refers to the
fact that, while in the ordinary sequence of the five agents Metal is the
mother of Water, Neidan inverts inverts the sequence: Water generates
Metal, the True Yang principle that will form the Elixir.

2. *Wuzhen pian*, "Lüshi," poem 7 (see Pregadio, *Awakening*, p. 42).

3. I have not identified the source of these verses, but similar sentences are found in many Neidan texts.

4. These verses are attributed to Zhongli Quan in the *Jinlian zheng-zong ji* (Records of the Correct Lineage of the Golden Lotus), ch. 1. This work, dating from the mid-thirteenth century, contains biographies of Quanzhen patriarchs and early masters. Zhongli Quan is one of most renowned Taoist Immortals. Around the tenth century he was placed at the origins of the Zhong-Lü tradition of Neidan, and was later accepted by Quanzhen Taoism as one if its foremost patriarchs.

5. *Wuzhen pian*, "Lüshi," poem 10 (see Pregadio, *Awakening*, p. 52).

6. In the form translated above, this verse derives from Chen Nan's *Cuixu pian* (The Emerald Emptiness). Wang Jie's text reads, "The one ingredient in the Flowery Pond (*huachi*) is Metal within Water."

12

The Opening of going back to the root,
the Barrier of returning to destiny.
Pierce through the Caudal Funnel,
pass through the Muddy Pellet.[1]

In the wondrous operation of compounding the Elixir, it is essential to understand the One Opening of the Mysterious Barrier.[2] In the true position of the One Nature, the ten thousand things go back to their root; and the Way of returning to one's destiny necessarily revolves through the Three Barriers.[3] Therefore it says, "the Opening of going back to the root, the Barrier of returning to destiny."

When you return to your destiny, you cause Spirit to "fly from the bottom of the sea,"[4] and maintain the Fire so that it produces steam. When the Essence transmutes itself into Breath, you turn the gear of the barrier in the sinciput. Slowly, ascending from the Caudal Funnel, [Breath] reaches the Muddy Pellet, and the conjunction [of Breath and Spirit] occurs.[5] When the Breath transmutes itself and becomes Spirit, this Spirit dwells in the Muddy Pellet, which is its own Palace; thus the ten thousand spirits go to have audience with it. Therefore it says, "pierce through the Caudal Funnel, pass through the Muddy Pellet."

The "Concealed Teachings" ("Aozhi") by the True Lord Wang (i.e., Wang Zihua) says:

> From the Caudal Funnel, crossing the Three Barriers, you
>   pass through the sinciput:
> holding a flower in its mouth, a white deer seems to walk
>   on the clouds.

> Grab the flower, ride the deer, and leave treading the
> clouds:
> then a chart pulled by an ox that ploughs the land will
> approach you and greet you.[6]

The *Huangting jing* (Scripture of the Yellow Court) says:

> If you wish to be free from death, cultivate Mount
> Kunlun.[7]

The *Huanyuan pian* (Returning to the Origin) says:

> In full radiance you awaken to the Dao, and a light illumi-
> nates the empty space:
> sit steady and relaxed, and set in motion the Barriers of
> Heaven.[8]

The *Daode jing* says:

> Going back to the root is called quiescence,
> being quiescent is called returning to one's destiny.[9]

This is what their discourses mean.

Notes

1. The first two verses of this stanza derive from the passage of the
Daode jing quoted at the end of the commentary to this section.

2. The One Opening of the Mysterious Barrier (*xuanguan yiqiao*) is
the Center of the human being and the cosmos, and the invisible but
ever-present point of conjunction between the Dao and our world.
Several Neidan masters therefore emphasize that this Opening is not to
be found either "inside" or "outside" oneself. In one of his other works
(*Huanzhen ji*, ch. 1), Wang Jie writes:

> The One Opening of the Mysterious Barrier is the exact and
>   correct Center:
> it is not in the back, not in the front — it reclines solitary onto
>   Emptiness.
> Silently revert your Light and let it dwell there:
> Spirit and Breath will merge into Mysterious Unity.

3. On the Three Barriers see section 14, note 2.

4. The Neidan use of the term "bottom of the sea" (*haidi*) derives from the *Wuzhen pian* ("Jueju," poem 19): "On the top of Mount Hua, the male Tiger roars; near the Fusang tree, at the bottom of the sea, the female Dragon howls." The "bottom of the sea" is the Water (Yin, the state of quiescence) from which Fire (Yang, Spirit) emerges.

5. The Caudal Funnel (*weilü*) is one of the "three barriers," located in the lowest section of the spine.

6. The work by Wang Zihua (714–89) cited by Wang Jie is now lost, but these verses are also quoted in the *Daofa huiyuan* (A Collection of Sources of Taoist Methods), ch. 76. Here the first verse reads, "From the double barrier of the Caudal Funnel, it enters Mount Kunlun," and there are minor variants also in other verses. — In Neidan, the chariot driven by the deer (*luche*) represents the vehicle that makes it possible to rise from the second to the third "barrier" in the back of the body. The chart pulled by the ox (*niuche*) makes it possible to proceed from the third "barrier" to the upper Cinnabar Field. See Wang Mu, *Foundations of Internal Alchemy*, pp. 83–84.

7. *Huangting jing*, "Outer" version, sec. 1. Mount Kunlun is a name of the upper Cinnabar Field.

8. These verses appear to be quoted from Zhang Wumeng's (952–1051) *Huanyuan pian*, a work now lost except for short quotations found in the *Daoshu* (Pivot of the Dao), ch. 12.

9. *Daode jing*, sec. 16.

13

The true bellows and nozzles,
the true tripod and furnace.
Being within Non-Being,
Non-Being within Being.

The bellows is an empty tool; it is a bag filled with air. The nozzles are the pipes; they are the openings. This concerns the Breath exhaled and inhaled by a person during the day and the night. This Breath acts like the wind in the venting mechanism of a furnace: as the wind is emitted from the pipes, the fire of the furnace blazes. In due time, Heart and breathing depend on one another, and the Cinnabar Field is constantly warm. These are the "true bellows and nozzles" in one's own body. This is what the *Daode jing* means when it says:

> The space between Heaven and Earth —
> is it not like a bellows?
> As empty, it is never exhausted;
> as it moves, it continues to pour.[1]

The tripod is Qian ☰ and is one's Nature. The furnace is Kun ☷ and is one's Existence. After you activate the bellows and nozzles in your own body, you must collect the ingredients and place them in the Tripod. When you collect them, you apply the function of the fierce Fire, so that your Nature is at work within and your Existence operates outside. In the blink of an eye, Qian and Kun become one, and Spirit and Breath conjoin. They coalesce and form the Reverted Elixir, which is the Embryo of Sainthood. Therefore it says, "the true tripod and furnace."

After you have been able to achieve the image of the Reverted Elixir, you should warmly nourish it by a gentle Fire.[2] Empty your heart to guard your Nature, and fill your belly to nourish your Existence.[3] In the "vague and indistinct," in the "dim and obscure,"[4] Being is born within Non-Being, and Non-Being is born within Being. This means that when quiescence culminates there is again movement, and when movement culminates there is again quiescence. Therefore it says, "Being within Non-Being, Non-Being within Being."

Notes

1. *Daode jing*, sec. 5.

2. In Taoism, the emergence of the "image" (*xiang*) is the initial stage in the generation of individual entities. For entities pertaining to the "world of form," this stage is followed by the emergence of "form" (*xing*), the principle of individuality through which each entity is distinguished by all others. The last stage is the emergence of "matter" (or "concrete substance," *zhi*).

3. *Daode jing*, sec. 3: "Thus the saint in his government empties the people's hearts and fills their bellies" ("heart" here is close in sense to "mind"). This passage of the *Daode jing* has often been used in Neidan with regard to the cultivation of Nature ("emptying the heart") and of Existence ("filling the belly"). The textual support for this association is a poem in the *Wuzhen pian* ("Jueju," no. 20):

> Empty the heart, fill the belly: the meanings are both profound.
> It is only in order to empty the heart that you should know the
>   heart.
> When refining Lead, nothing is better than first filling
>   the belly;
> then, by guarding and collecting, you load the hall with Gold.

4. *Daode jing*, sec. 21: "Vague and indistinct! Within there is something. Dim and obscure! Within there is an essence."

14

Count on the Yellow Dame
as match-maker for the Lovely Maid.
Lightly,
silently, it rises.

Yellow Dame and Lovely Maid are names used by necessity.[1] The
Yellow Dame is the Kun ☷ Soil, that is, the Soil of *wu* and *ji*; it is
also called the Intention. The Lovely Maid is the Dui ☱ Metal;
Dui is the youngest daughter, and Metal hides Water within itself.

When you compound the Elixir, you must always count on the
Yellow Dame as the match-maker, as she thoroughly understands
the feelings of the Lovely Maid: the *wu* (Yang) Soil stores Fire,
and Fire forces Metal into movement. When you begin to kindle
the Fire, the Breath (*qi*) received [by the Lovely Maid] is still
weak. You should turn the gear of the barrier in the sinciput, and
let [the Fire] rise "lightly, silently" from the Caudal Cavity. Suddenly the force of Fire becomes intense, and the River Chariot
cannot be halted.[2] After [the Lovely Maid] enters the Southern
Palace, she returns to the original position.[3] [Then] she "marries
the Lord of Metals making him an old gentleman."[4]

Master Cui earnestly warns us and urges us. Thinking that the
people of this world would not realize the teachings on the Reverted Elixir, he uses the metaphor of "counting on the Yellow
Dame as a match-maker for the Lovely Maid," only because he
wished that everyone comprehends this principle.

This is what the *Wuzhen pian* means when it says:

> The roaming of the Lovely Maid follows set directions:
>   her journey in the front takes a shorter time, and the one
>   in the back, a longer time.

Coming back, she enters the Yellow Dame's dwelling,
and marries the Lord of Metals making him an old gentleman.[5]

Notes

1. Lit., "forced names" (*qiangming*). This expression alludes to the famous passage in the *Daode jing*, sec. 25, that says: "I do not know its name, but call it Dao; if I am forced to give it a name, I say 'great.'"

2. The term River Chariot (*heche*) has multiple meanings in Neidan. Here it denotes the route formed by the Function and Control vessels (*renmai* and *dumai*, in the front and the back of the body, respectively), through which a "chariot" transports the ingredients of the Elixir. Along the back of this route—where one proceeds by "inverting the course" (*ni*)—are found the "three barriers" (*sanguan*), i.e., the Caudal Funnel (*weilü*), the Spinal Handle (*jiaji*), and the Jade Pillow (*yuzhen*). Along its front—where one proceeds by "following the course" (*shun*)—are found the three Cinnabar Fields. See Wang Mu, *Foundations of Internal Alchemy*, pp. 71–74.

3. The Southern Palace (*nangong*) here is upper Cinnabar Field. (Note that in traditional Chinese cartography, the south is placed "above," and the north is placed "below.")

4. These words derive from the *Wuzhen pian* poem quoted at the end of the commentary to the present section.

5. *Wuzhen pian*, "Jueju," poem 26 (see Cleary, *Understanding Reality*, p. 83). The journey "in the back" is longer, because the Lovely Maid ascends from the Caudal Funnel to the upper Cinnabar Field by "inverting the course." The journey "in the front" is shorter, because she descends from the upper to the lower Cinnabar Fields by "following the course."

15

Within one day,
during the twelve hours,
wherever the Intention goes,
all can be done.

The Intention is the operation of one's Nature; it is the True Soil. Within the twelve [double] hours of one day there are the time phases of a whole year. The six [hours] from *zi* to *chen* and *si* pertain to Yang; the six [hours] from *wu* to *xu* and *hai* pertain to Yin.[1] When the initial Yang returns with Fu ䷗, it is the time of *zi* within the body; when the initial Yin is born with Gou ䷫, it is the time of *wu* within the body.

However, Water and Fire are divided between North and South, and Wood and Metal are separated between East and West. How can these four images be joined? You must avail yourself of the Intention in order to move through the ebb and the flow.[2] By doing so, in a while you can seize the creation and transformation of Heaven and Earth.

In the twelve [double] hours of one day there is no daytime or nighttime; concentrate on this, examine it, and always be watchful. When your thoughts are in motion, the Fire circulates; when you pause them, the Fire nourishes warmly. This is why it says, "wherever the Intention goes, all can be done."

Notes

1. In other words, the first six earthly branches (*dizhi*), i.e., *zi* 子, *chou* 丑, *yin* 寅, *mao* 卯, *chen* 辰, and *si* 巳, represent the Yang part of

the day, while the last six, i.e., *wu* 午, *wei* 未, *shen* 申, *you* 酉, *xu* 戌, and *hai* 亥, represent its second part. In premodern China, the day was divided into twelve "hours" (*shi*), corresponding to two hours in modern reckoning.

2. "Ebb and flow" (*xiaoxi*) refers to the two main parts of time cycles of any length. The first half is marked by the growth of the Yang principle, and the second half by the decrease of the Yang principle and the parallel growth of the Yin principle. In the previous paragraph, Wang Jie refers to the two halves as the times of Fu and Gou. Other illustrations of this pattern are found in Wang Jie's commentary to sections 2, on the cycle of the Moon, and 16, on the "starting point" and the "midpoint." In Neidan, the ebb and flow of the time cycles is reproduced by the Fire Phases.

16

Swallow a knife-point,
peep into the skill of Heaven.
Distinguish the starting point and the midpoint,
comprehend dawn and dusk.

"To swallow" means "to have one's fill"; the "knife" means the Metal within Water; the "point" means the True Soil of *wu* and *ji*.¹ This means that when you collect the ingredients to compound the Elixir, you must collect the Metal within the Water. If the Metal cannot ascend of its own, you must avail yourself of the transforming Fire of the *wu* (Yang) Soil, and force the Metal into movement so that it advances up to the Muddy Pellet. When it arrives there, the Metal transmutes itself into True Liquor, which is similar to the Jasper Wine and the Sweet Dew.² As one drop of it falls into the Yellow Court, have your fill of it and taste it: it is sweet and delightful. Therefore it says, "swallow a knife-point."

"To peep" means to contemplate. This means that if you can contemplate the operation of the cyclical transformations of the Way of Heaven, and if you can hold to the operation of Heaven, you revolve the mechanism of the Dipper's Handle in your own body, and in a while you seize the creation and transformation of Heaven and Earth. Therefore it says, "peep into the skill of Heaven." This is what the *Yinfu jing* (Scripture of the Hidden Agreement) means when it says:

> Contemplate the Way of Heaven, hold to the operation of Heaven: this is completeness.³

And this is what a poem by Chunyang (i.e., Lü Dongbin) means when it says:

Moving unhindered across the Northern Dipper, the
  mechanism of the mind is skilled;
turning the Southern Constellation upside down, its bold-
  ness is impressive.[4]

As for "distinguishing the starting point and the midpoint,"
with regard to the year, the winter solstice is the starting point
and the summer solstice is the midpoint; with regard to the
month, the 1st day is the starting point and the 15th day is the
midpoint; with regard to the day, the *zi* hour is the starting point
and the *wu* hour is the midpoint; with regard to the [double]
hour, the first quarter is the starting point and the fifth quarter is
the midpoint; with regard to the sixty-four hexagrams, the Fu ䷗
hexagram is the starting point and the Gou ䷫ hexagram is the
midpoint; with regard to the human body, the Caudal Cavity is
the starting point and the Muddy Pellet is the midpoint; "advancing the Fire from the Palace of *zi*" is the starting point and "withdrawing in response from the position of *wu*" is the midpoint.[5]

After you understand this principle, you must comprehend
"dawn and dusk." "Dusk" means the evening; "dawn" means the
morning. Among the hexagrams there is the principle of "Zhun
䷂ in the morning and Meng ䷃ in the evening." One hexagram
has six lines; by turning it upside down, there are two
hexagrams.[6] With "Zhun ䷂ in the morning," the initial Yang is
born below; with "Meng ䷃ in the evening," the initial Yin is born
above.[7] One Yin and one Yang, once advancing and once withdrawing: the cyclical transformations in the human body are the
same as those of Heaven and Earth.[8]

When you realize this principle, you can live a long life and
have a lasting presence; you will be on a par with Zhongli Quan
and Lü Dongbin, and will converse with them as their
companion. Do you have any doubts?

Notes

1. *Daogui*, translated above as "knife-point," more precisely means "tip of a spatula." This term derives from Waidan (External Alchemy), where the spatula is the tool used to collect the elixir from the vessel, and one ingests "a tip" of it. In the Neidan interpretation of this term followed by Wang Jie, *dao* ("blade, spatula, knife") alludes to Metal, whose "mother" in the system of the five agents is Water. *Gui* 圭 stands for the "two Soils 土" (one on top of the other), representing the Yin and Yang aspects of Soil that are incorporated into the Elixir. In other words, in Neidan "knife-point" becomes a synonym of "elixir."

2. The name Jasper Wine (*qiongjiang*) derives from the "Zhaohun" ("Summoning the *Hun*-Soul") poem in the *Songs of Chu* (*Chuci*), where this drink is offered to the soul of the deceased in order to entice it to return to life. The name Sweet Dew (*ganlu*) derives from the *Daode jing*, sec. 32, which says that, in ancient times, "Heaven and Earth joined to one another, causing thereby the Sweet Dew to descend."

3. *Yinfu jing*, sec. 1.

4. The original text containing these verses appears to be lost. In his commentary to the *Yinfu jing*, Wang Jie quotes these verses again as coming from a "Jindan shi" ("Poem on the Golden Elixir"), attributed to Lü Dongbin.

5. All the examples given by Wang Jie in this paragraph concern the stages of increase and decrease of the Yin and Yang principles during time cycles of different length (in particular, the day, the month, and the year). These cycles are reproduced within the human body by the circuit that begins from the Caudal Cavity (at the bottom of the spine), rises on the back of the body, culminates in the Muddy Pellet (the upper Cinnabar Field), and then descends on the front of the body, going through the middle Cinnabar Field and ending in the lower Cinnabar Field. The "Palace of *zi*" is the Caudal Cavity (the "starting point"), and the "position of *wu*" is the Muddy Pellet (the "midpoint").

6. The hexagrams of the *Book of Changes* are arranged into pairs, formed either by inverting the solid and broken lines of the first hexagram (e.g., Qian ䷀ is followed by Kun ䷁) or by turning the first hexagram upside down (e.g., Zhun ䷂ is followed by Meng ䷃). Zhun ䷂ and Meng ䷃, the first and second hexagrams after Qian and Kun, respectively correspond to daytime and nighttime of the month's first day.

7. "Above" does not refer to the image of Meng ䷃ (where the Yin line is at the bottom), but to the midpoint of the cycle, which begins "below" and culminates "above."

8. This paragraph concerns the cycle of the day, which is the third main cosmological cycle on which the Neidan practice of the Fire Phases is based. Each day is associated with two hexagrams, which represent the growth of the Yang principle during daytime, and the growth of the Yin principle during nighttime. For Neidan, the classical description of this cycle is found in sec. 3 of the *Cantong qi* (see Pregadio, *The Seal of the Unity of the Three*, pp. 69–70, and table 7 on p. 252). Wang Jie has mentioned the other two main cycles—those of the month and the year—in his notes on sec. 2 of the *Mirror*.

17

Comprehend the floating and the sinking,
understand the host and the guest.
You must gather them and bring them together:
do not let them separate.[1]

What floats is Mercury; what sinks is Lead. The Li ☲ Mercury
dwelling above is said to be "floating," the Kan ☵ Lead dwelling
below is said to be "sinking." According to the instructions for
cultivating the Elixir, what sinks must ascend, and what floats
must descend. Therefore it says, "comprehend the floating and
the sinking."

After you "comprehend the floating and the sinking," you must
"understand the host and the guest." The host is one's Existence;
the guest is one's Nature. When there is a body there is Existence,
when there is Existence there is Nature. Nature is established by
complying with Existence, and Existence is cultivated by means
of Nature. Therefore Existence is the mother of Nature, and thus
is the host; Nature is the child of Existence, and thus is the guest.
Day after day they operate by means of the body. This is what our
Immortal Master (i.e., Zhang Boduan) meant when he said, "Let
the other be the host, and you are the guest."[2]

After you "understand the host and the guest," place Lead and
Mercury in the same furnace, and the host and the guest in the same
chamber. "Unceasingly and continuously," during the two sets of six
hours, reverse the light and invert the radiance.[3] As [Lead and
Mercury] become one thing, they entirely fill the Great Emptiness.[4]

When the time comes and Breath transmutes itself, the mechanism moves and the pipes resound;[5] Fire comes forth under the
navel, and Water is born within the sinciput. The wonder of this
lies in its happening of its own and at an unexpected time.

Confucius said:

> The Dao is that from which you cannot separate even for
> one instant. If you can separate from it, it is not the Dao.[6]

Master Cheng (i.e., Cheng Yi) said:

> Keep your heart within the chest.[7]

And the Celestial Master Xujing (i.e., Zhang Jixian) said:

> If the Spirit leaves, collect it at once:
> as it returns to the body, Breath comes back of its own.
> Do this every morning, do it every evening,
> and the Red Child will be born of its own in the Numi-
> nous Womb.[8]

This is why it says, "you must gather them and bring them together: do not let them separate."

Notes

1. For the first two verses of this stanza, compare *Wuzhen pian*,
"Lüshi," poem 4: "I know for myself how to invert, starting from Li ☲
and Kan ☵. Who else can comprehend the floating and the sinking, and
determine the host and the guest?" (see Pregadio, *Awakening*, p. 31).

2. *Wuzhen pian*, "Jueju," poem 23 (see Cleary, *Understanding
Reality*, p. 81).

3. "Unceasingly and continuously" derives from the *Daode jing*, sec.
6 (translated above in the commentary on sec. 1). "Reversing the light
and inverting the radiance" (*huiguang fanzhao*) means turning the
direction of one's brightness, so that it illuminates within instead of
being dispersed outside. This is also the name of the practice made
illustrious, in the later Neidan tradition, by the *Secret of the Golden
Flower* (*Jinhua zongzhi*), where one's light is circulated within the body.
This passage of Wang Jie's commentary shows that the practice already
existed at an earlier time.

4. For this sentence, I follow the text in the *Daozang jiyao*. The

Daozang edition has, "As [Lead and Mercury] become one thing, the Dao fills the Great Emptiness."

5. Wang Jie borrows this expression from Yu Yan's commentary to the *Cantong qi*, where it occurs repeatedly (*Zhouyi cantong qi fahui*, ch. 5. 7, and 9). The sentence may allude to the "pipes of Heaven" of the *Zhuangzi*, ch. 2, which "blow on the ten thousand things in a different way, so that each can be itself" (see Watson, *The Complete Works of Chuang-tzu*, p. 36).

6. *Zhongyong* (The Doctrine of the Mean), sec. 1 (see Legge, *Confucian Analects, The Great Learning, and The Doctrine of the Mean*, p. 384).

7. *Er Cheng yishu* (Writings Bequeathed by the Cheng Brothers), ch. 7. The full sentence in this work is: "If you want to exit the cage, keep your heart in the chest," where "in the chest" means "in its proper place." Cheng Yi (1033–1107) and his brother Cheng Hao (1032–85) were two of the main Neo-Confucian thinkers.

8. Zhang Jixian (1092–1126) was the thirtieth Celestial Master (*tianshi*). These verses are quoted from his *Sanshi dai tianshi Xujing zhenjun yulu* (Recorded Sayings of the Thirtieth Generation Celestial Master, True Lord of Empty Quiescence), ch. 3.

18

When you collect the ingredients,
harmonize the function of Fire.
Receive the fortune of Breath,
avoid that it results in misfortune.

"When you collect the ingredients" means the time when the
initial Yang within yourself returns. At that time, you must close
the barriers. In the function of circulating Fire, the wonder lies in
harmonizing and maintaining the continuity. [Fire] revolves
through the Three Barriers, and each of its rises spans three time-
units (*shi*).[1] After it flows through a complete cycle, it returns to
its position, and the ten thousand breaths coagulate and become
true. At that time, all you experience is freedom and happiness in
your own spirit, a delight that can hardly be expressed in words.
Therefore it says, "receive the fortune of Breath."

In "circulating the Fire and withdrawing in response," the
main point lies in maintaining sincerity (*cuncheng*), which cannot
be interrupted for one instant.[2] If there is an error as fine as a
hair, this results in misfortune. You must use the greatest attention and you must protect yourself; you cannot be careless. This is
the operation of "avoiding dangers in the fight in the wild";
therefore it says, "avoid that it results in misfortune."[3]

A scripture on the Elixir says:

Mate Tiger and Dragon in the place of conjunction:
at that time, act as if you are crossing a narrow bridge.[4]

There is someone who says: "As for quiescence of Nature and
non-doing, if you want to sit then just sit, and if you want to
sleep then just sleep. What need is there to be skillful in collecting
the ingredients and harmonizing the Fire?" Well, if someone does

not know that there are creation and transformation, it is point-less to discuss with them.

Notes

1. This expression seems to mean that Fire goes through four "rises," each of which has a symbolic duration of three time-units marked by the Earthly Branches, namely: (1) from *zi* (the Caudal Funnel) to *yin*; (2) from *mao* (the first "bathing") to *si*; (3) from *wu* (the Muddy Pellet) to *shen*; (4) from *you* (the second "bathing") to *hai*. Note that *juhuo* is a classical expression meaning "to raise (*or*: to kindle) the fire."

2. On "maintaining sincerity" see above, section 7 note 5. For "one instant," here Wang Jie uses the Buddhist expression *yinian*, lit., "one thought."

3. On the "fight in the wild" see above, section 7 note 6.

4. These verses are quoted from Xiao Tingzhi's *Jindan da chengji*, in *Xiuzhen shishu*, ch. 11.

19

The Fire Phases are sufficient:
do not harm the Elixir.
Heaven and Earth are numinous,
creation and transformation are mean.

Through the refining, the Yellow Sprout fills the Tripod, the White Snow pervades Heaven, and the Infant achieves an image. Therefore "the Fire Phases are sufficient."[1]

When the Fire Phases are sufficient, you only have to "bathe" and "nourish warmly." If you do not know how to stop when it is sufficient, and with errant intention you [continue to] circulate the Fire, this would harm the Elixir.[2] After the Elixir has been formed, Heaven and Earth will be inchoately merged, and Breath and Spirit will be numinous of their own. This is what the Immortal Masters meant when they said, "in the empty chamber, brightness is born,"[3] and "the Numinous Light will come of its own."[4] Therefore it says, "Heaven and Earth are numinous."

At that time, you must provide protection and love. In harmonizing breathing, the main point lies in making it subtle and fine. In quiescence and concentration, what is inside does not exit, and what is outside does not enter. Forms are forgotten, things are forgotten. The Heart is equal to the Great Emptiness, in the Pure Yang of the One Breath. Therefore "creation and transformation are mean."[5]

Notes

1. The Yellow Sprout (*huangya*) and the White Snow (*baixue*) represent the True Yang and the True Yin principles, respectively.

2. The important Neidan doctrine of "knowing when to stop" (*zhizhi*) or "knowing what is sufficient" (*zhizu*) has antecedents in both Taoism and Confucianism. For Taoism, see *Daode jing*, sec. 44: "Know what is sufficient and you will not be disgraced; know when to stop and you will not be in danger"; and *Daode jing*, sec. 46: "There is no calamity greater than not knowing what is sufficient." For Confucianism, see *Daxue* (The Great Learning), sec. 2: "Only if you know when to stop there is stability; and only if there is stability there is quiescence" (see Legge, p. 356).

3. *Zhuangzi*, ch. 4: "Look into that closed room, the empty chamber where brightness is born!" (Watson, p. 58).

4. *Cantong qi*, 22:2: "Know the white, keep to the black, and the Numinous Light will come of its own" (Pregadio, *The Seal*, p. 78).

5. "Creation and transformation" are "mean" (or "miserly, impoverished," *qian*) because multiplicity has been brought back to the state of Unity.

20

As you first coalesce the Embryo,
watch your fundamental destiny.
As you finally deliver the Embryo,
watch the four cardinal points.

The primordial root of Heaven resides in the middle of the Inchoate: it is the place where you coalesce the Embryo. From the
moment in which you start to practice, refine the Essence to
transmute it into Breath, refine the Breath to transmute it into
Spirit, refine the Spirit to transmute it into Emptiness, and refine
the Emptiness to join with the Dao. [Thus] you coalesce the
Embryo of Sainthood.

When you first coalesce the Embryo, you should constantly
guard it in your Stem of Destiny (*mingdi*).[1] Therefore it says, "as
you first coalesce the Embryo, watch your fundamental destiny."

"In ten months the embryo is complete";[2] you move the Spirit
to dwell above in the Muddy Pellet, and harmonize it in order to
"exit the shell."[3] Just wait until your work is achieved and your
practice is concluded, and the Emperor on High will summon
you.[4] You will smash Emptiness and will rise on high as a True
Man (*zhenren*), mounting the red clouds and riding a white crane.
In the East, the West, the South, and the North there will be no
place where you cannot go. Therefore it says, "as you finally
deliver the Embryo, watch the four cardinal points."

This is what the "Jingzhong yin" ("Chant of Quiescence in the
Center") means when it says:

> One day the work was concluded, but no one else knew it,
> and all of me became like a tower enlightened by the
> midnight light.[5]

Notes

1. As a locus in the physical body, the Stem of Destiny (or Stem of Life, *mingdi*) is sometimes equated with the navel. More broadly, however, this term denotes the lower Cinnabar Field, just like the corresponding term Root of Nature (*xinggeng*) denotes the upper Cinnabar Field, but is sometimes equated with the sinciput.

2. *Wuzhen pian*, "Lüshi," poem 14: "In ten months the embryo is complete — this is the foundation for entering sainthood" (see Pregadio, *Awakening*, p. 63).

3. On "harmonizing the Spirit" (*tiaoshen*) see Wang Mu, *Foundations of Internal Alchemy*, pp. 56–59. "Exiting the shell" (*chuqiao*) denotes the moment in which the Embryo leaves its womb.

4. Compare *Cantong qi*, 27:9–12: "With the Way completed and virtue fulfilled, withdraw, stay concealed, and wait for your time. The Great One will send forth his summons, and you move your abode to the Central Land" (see Pregadio, *The Seal*, p. 82).

5. These verses have been variously attributed to Shi Jianwu (fl. 820–35) or to Chen Nan (?–1213), but are not found in their respective texts in the Taoist Canon.

21

Practice this word by word,
it will respond sentence by sentence.[1]

These two verses summarize the previous eighty verses. They mean that in the Great Way of the Golden Elixir, "advancing the Fire and withdrawing in response" are the wondrous instructions on seizing creation and transformation.[2] When they are practiced, the whole person becomes like an empty valley that responds to a sound, or like the *yangsui* mirror that collects Water and the *fangzhu* mirror that collects Fire.[3] Spirit pervades and Breath responds: could anything happen faster than this? Therefore it says, "practice this word by word, it will respond sentence by sentence."

A scripture on the Elixir says:

> Watching, you do not see it, listening, you do not
>   hear it —
> but if you call it, it responds.

Notes

1. *Mimi* means "closely." I translate "word by word" to preserve the parallelism with the next verse.

2. In this sentence, I read *jindan dadao* for *dadao jindan*, which would mean, "the Golden Elixir of the Great Way."

3. These images derive from the *Cantong qi*, 67:2 and 57:1–4, respectively (see Pregadio, *The Seal*, pp. 107 and 102). The *yangsui* mirror is round like Heaven, and receives the essence of the Yang

principle (fire) sent forth by the Sun; the *fangzhu* mirror is square like the Earth, and gathers the essence of the Yin principle (water or dew) sent forth by the Moon. These mirrors were used in early Taoist meditation practices and in several other contexts.

Five Poems by Wang Jie

"Shown on a Golden Placard"

Translator's note: At the end of his commentary, Wang Jie adds five poems that present the whole Neidan process as occurring during the five "vigils" (*geng*) of the night (formally corresponding to 7–9pm, 9–11pm, 11pm–1am, 1–3am, and 3–5am). The title of the poems alludes to the nomination of the adept as immortal: at that time, his name is inscribed on a golden placard.

1

At the first vigil you sit steady;
as you start to practice, harmonize the Original Breath.
In the Inchoate there are no words,
you stop your thoughts and maintain the True Intention.
Exhalation and inhalation are unceasing and continuous;
they conjoin and dwell in the Center.
Just open the barrier a little:
one grain of millet stores Heaven and Earth.

2

At the second vigil you are clear and pure;
constantly guard your Heart in Emptiness.
Silently reverse the Light,
and in the radiance you will see Being within Non-Being.
Driving away all the demons,
shaking the earth, the Golden Lion roars.
In one instant your work is completed:
you will live as long as Heaven.

3

At the third vigil the cock crows;
at the winter solstice the Yang first moves.
Taking from Kan to fill Li,
you send it straight to the Muddy Pellet.
Fire circulates for one celestial revolution,
within the furnace Lead seizes Mercury.
In nine cycles the Elixir is achieved:
the White Snow flies in the cave of the Immortals.

4

At the fourth vigil you are peaceful and untroubled;
you give no thought to the ten thousand pursuits.
Water fills the Flowery Pond,
it irrigates the Numinous Root and allows it to grow.
Quiescence holds Qian and Kun,
the music of the Immortals resounds again and again.
In the greatness of the Dao, you surge into Emptiness:
your name is shown on a golden placard.

5

At the fifth vigil the Moon falls;
gradually you are aware of the dawn in the east.
The True Man of the Valley
has already comprehended all.
At the Jade Gate there is a chariot of phoenixes,
on the Golden Peak, the dragons are coiled.
You smash Void and Emptiness:
ten thousand rays of golden light shine.

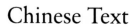

Chinese Text

崔公入藥鏡註解

王玠

神仙之學，豈凡夫俗子之可聞。必是大根大器決烈丈夫、明眼高士之可為也。且夫學者為者何事？外則窮天地施化之理，內則明身心運用之機。然雖如是，宣尼若不遇老子親授，故無猶龍之歎。瞿曇不是古聖再來，豈有出世之見。所以學者如牛毛，達者如麟角。此無他，在乎得傳與不得傳耳。神仙之學，不過修鍊性命，返本還源而已。採先天一炁以為丹母，運後天之氣以行火候。以火煉性，則金神不壞。以火鍊其命，則道氣長存。換盡陰濁之軀，變成純陽之體，神化自在，應運無窮，豈不奇哉。余見其今之學仙者紛紛之多，及至與其辯論真訣，人各偏執一見，不合先師正傳之道。觀其《崔公入藥鏡》八十二句，言簡而意盡，貫穿諸丹經之骨髓。予不愧管窺之見，遂將吾師所授口訣，每四句下添一註腳，剖露玄機，作人天眼目。後之來與我同志，試留心玩誦，斷斷有神告心悟之效無疑也。或者有云吾註不足為信，而崔公之言當以為實，依而行之，信而從之，運鍊一身，則學仙之能事畢矣。修江混然子序。

1

先天炁，後天炁。得之者，常似醉。

先天炁者，乃元始祖炁也。此祖炁在人身天地之正中，生門密戶，懸中高處，天心是也。神仙修鍊，止是採取先天一炁，以為

丹母。後天炁者，乃一呼一吸，一往一來，內運之炁也。呼則接
天根，吸則接地根；呼則龍吟而雲起，吸則虎嘯而風生。綿綿若
存，歸于祖炁，內外混合，結成還丹。自覺丹田火熾，暢於四
肢。如癡如醉，美在其中。此所以「得之者，常似醉」也。《道
德經》云：「谷神不死，是謂玄牝。玄牝之門，是為天地根。綿
綿若存，用之不勤」，《易・坤卦》云：「黃中通理，正位居
體，美在其中，而暢於四肢」。如斯之謂也。

2

日有合，月有合。窮戊己，定庚甲。

日月者，太陽太陰也。天有黃道，為度三百六十五度四之一，其
運轉也，一日一周，日月行乎其間。往來上下，迭為出入，此所
以分晝夜而定寒暑也。當冬至之節，一陽生于復，日從北行，月
從南行。夏至之節，一陰生于姤，日從南行，月從北行。日行一
日一度，至三十度，與太陰會。月本無光，借日之光。月行一日
十二度有零，至三十日，行滿周天之度。每月晦朔，與太陽同會
所行之宮，日月合（壁）〔璧〕，晦象年終，朔象歲首，會而復
離，離而復還。月因日以受其明，陽魂漸長，陰魄漸消。至初八
日夜，陽半陰半為上弦；至十五日夜，與日對照，為望故圓。圓
滿之極，其理當虧，于是陰魄漸長，陽魂漸消。至二十三日夜，
陰半陽半為下弦；至三十日夜為晦，又復與日同會。此天之「日
有合，月有合」也。反求於身，吾身一天地，亦有日月也。以身
為乾坤，以坎離為藥物，以日月運行為火候。百姓日用而不知，
豈知行之！吾身與天地日月無不同也。當作丹之時，運日月之雙
輪，簇陰陽於一息，日月歸鼎，陰陽構精，烹之煉之，結成聖
胎。此吾身「日有合、月有合」也。了真子曰：「玉池常滴陰陽
髓，金鼎時烹日月精」，是也。既明日月之合，必窮戊己之源。
戊己者，中央土也。水火分為上下，木金列於東西。木為火母，
金為水母，若非戊己之功，水火不能既濟，金木不得歸併。當施

化之際，是用戊土從坎起，進之以陽火，己土從離降，退之以陰符。攝回四象而同爐。此戊己之功也。既窮戊己之理，必定庚甲之方。庚西方，金也、情也、虎也。甲東方，木也、性也、龍也。言人之情，好於馳騁，見物即逐，如虎猖狂，故每傷於性。性被情迷，不能為主，如龍奔騰。故二物間隔。大修行人，制之不難。遇此時，正好下手施功。須仗黃婆媒合，旋斗柄之機。一息之間，即得金木歸併，情性合一，龍虎入鼎，心虛湛然，此所以「定庚甲」也。丹家妙用，宜乎生甲生庚，學者不可不知也。

3

上鵲橋，下鵲橋。天應星，地應潮。

人身夾脊，比天之銀河也。銀河阻隔，而有靈鵲作橋，故有鵲橋之說。人之舌亦言鵲橋也。凡作丹之時，以黃婆引嬰兒上昇泥丸，與姹女交會，名曰「上鵲橋」也。黃婆復徘徊，笑引嬰兒姹女同歸洞房。必從泥丸而降，故曰「下鵲橋」也。黃婆、嬰兒、姹女非真有也，乃譬喻之說，無出乎身心意三者而已。默運之功，內仗天罡斡運，外用斗柄推遷。起火之時，覺真氣騰騰上昇，如潮水之初起，直上逆流。故曰「天應星、地應潮」也。丹經云：「工夫容易藥非遙」，「撥動天輪地應潮」，是也。

4

起巽風，運坤火。入黃房，成至寶。

作丹之法，乃鍊吾身中真鉛真汞也。鉛遇癸生之時，便當鼓動巽風，搧開爐鞴，運動坤宮之火，沉潛於下，抽出坎中之陽，去補離中之陰，成乾之象，復歸坤位而止。片餉之間，發火煅鍊，鉛清汞潔，結成空無金胎，歷劫不壞，此所以「入黃房，成至寶」也。《度人經》云：「中理五炁，混合百神，十轉迴靈，萬炁齊仙」。蕭廷芝云：「大藥三般精氣神，天然子母互相親，回風混合歸真體，煆鍊工夫日日新」，是也。

5

水怕乾，火怕寒。差毫髮，不成丹。

修真內鍊之要，鼎中之水不可乾，爐內之火不可寒。丹經所謂：「金鼎常留湯火煖，玉爐不要火教寒」，是也。以外丹言之，凡作丹之時，行武鍊文烹之功，大要調和火力。若用之太過，則火燥水（濫）〔乾〕，不及則水（乾）〔濫〕火寒，務在行之停勻。一刻周天，水火既濟，鼎內丹結，自然而然也。若差之毫髮不成丹矣。仙師云：「藥有老嫩，火有斤兩」，學者不可不知。了真子有云乎：「七返九還須識主，工夫毫髮不容差」，《悟真篇》云：「大都全藉修持力，毫髮差殊不作丹」，是也。

6

鉛龍昇，汞虎降。驅二物，勿縱放。

鉛者，坎中一點真陽，謂之龍也。汞者，離中一點真陰，謂之虎也。凡作丹之時，飛戊土抽坎中之鉛，木生火而炎，上昇泥丸，龍從火裏出，故曰「鉛龍昇」也。用己土攝離中之汞，金生水而流，下降丹田，虎向水中生，故曰「汞虎降」也。擒捉之功，非加武火之力，則鉛龍不昇。非用文火之力，則汞虎不降。一息周流妙在堅剛。著力擒龍虎入鼎，烹鍊化為玉漿。故曰「驅二物，勿縱放」也。張紫陽云：「西山白虎性猖狂，東海青龍不可當，兩手捉來令死鬪，鍊成一塊紫金霜」，是也。

7

產在坤，種在乾。但至誠，法自然。

張紫陽云：「要知產藥川源處，只在西南是本鄉」。此所以言吾身西南方，乃坤位也。人腹為坤，人首為乾，坤居下為爐，乾居上為鼎。金丹大藥「產在坤，種在乾」。凡作丹採藥之時，必從坤位發端，沉潛尾穴溫養。見龍當加武火，逼逐真陽之氣，逆上乾宮交姤，復還坤位而止，猛烹極煅，結成至寶。故曰「產在坤，種在乾」。其中復有先天產藥之時，觀心吸神，握定不泄，皆助火侯之力。古仙往往秘而不言，此最上機關，人誰知之？行持之間，唯在存誠。野戰防危，法天象地，應化自然。故曰：「但至誠，法自然」也。

8

盜天地，奪造化。攢五行，會八卦。

提挈天地，握定陰陽，攢簇五行，合會八卦，此神仙之學也。天地者，即乾坤也。造化者，即陰陽也。五行者，金木水火土也。八卦者，乾坤坎離震巽艮兌，是也。且夫天地之大，造化之深，五行分布，八卦環列，以何術能盜之奪之、攢之會之？盜者，竊也。奪者，取也。攢者，簇也。會者，合也。此言丹家之法，妙在口傳。凡作丹真訣，只在些兒消息。待時至氣化，藥產神知，便當閉風關，塞艮戶，斡天罡，旋斗柄，運符火之一息，簇三千六百之正炁，回七十二侯之要津。顛倒五行，會合八卦總歸土釜，牢固封閉。須臾調燮火發，武鍊猛烹，結成聖胎。所以一刻工夫，奪一年之節候。丹經云：「人心若與天心合，顛倒陰陽只片時」。此即一呼一吸能奪造化。人一日有一萬三千五百呼，一萬三千五百吸。一呼一吸為一息，則一息之間，潛奪天運一萬三千五百年之數。一年三百六十日四百八十六萬息，潛奪天運四百八十六萬年之數。於是換盡陰濁之軀，變成純陽之體。神化自在，聚則成形，散則成風，出有入無，隱顯莫測，豈不奇哉！

9

水真水，火真火。水火交，永不老。

水居北方，在卦為坎，在身為腎。火居南方，在卦為離，在身為心。水中藏火，火中藏水。人心中一點真液，乃真水也。腎中一點真陽，乃真火也。水火分於上下，何由而交之？必假戊己真土擒制逼逐，得其真火上昇，真水下降，同歸土釜。水火既濟，結成金丹，一炁純陽，與天齊壽。故曰「水火交，永不老」也。

10

水能流，火能燄。在身中，自可驗。

水在上，故能流潤於下；火在下，故能炎燄於上，此天地水火昇降自然之理。人身作丹，運用之時，亦復如是。故曰「在身中，自可驗」也。

11

是性命，非神氣。水鄉鉛，只一味。

性即神也，命即氣也。性命混合，乃先天之體也；神氣運化，乃後天之用也，故曰「是性命，非神氣」也。修鍊之士，欲得其性靈命固，從下手之初，必是採水鄉之鉛。水鄉鉛者，坤因乾破而為坎，坎水中而有乾金。「金為水母，母隱子胎」，一點真陽居於此處，遇身中子時陽動之際，急急採之。紫陽所謂「鉛遇癸生須急採」，採時須以徘徊之意。引火逼金，正所謂「火逼金行顛倒轉，自然鼎內大丹凝」。只此一味，為大道之根。雲房云：「生我之門死我戶，幾箇惺惺幾箇悟，夜來鐵漢細尋思，長生不死由人做」。指此一味，直欲世人於此尋之，方是鍊丹之本。丹經云：「好把真鉛著意尋」，「華池一味水中金」，是也。

12

歸根竅，復命關。貫尾閭，通泥丸。

作丹妙用，要明玄關一竅。一性正位，萬化歸根，復命之道，必由三關而轉。故曰「歸根竅，復命關」也。當復命之時，飛神海底，存火燻蒸。精化為氣，撥動頂門關捩，從尾閭徐徐提起，直上泥丸交姤。鍊氣化為神，神居泥丸為本宮，則有萬神朝會。故曰「貫尾閭，通泥丸」也。火師汪真君《奧旨》云：「夾脊三關透頂門，銜花騎鹿走如雲，捉花騎鹿踏雲去，霍地牛車前面迎」。《黃庭經》云：「子欲不死修崑崙」。《還元篇》云：「悟道顯然明廓落，閑閑端坐運天關」。《道德經》云：「歸根曰靜，靜曰復命」。其說是已。

13

真橐籥，真鼎爐。無中有，有中無。

橐者，虛器也，鞴也。籥者，其管也，竅也。言人晝夜一呼一吸之氣，氣為之風，如爐鞴之抽動，風生于管，爐火自炎，久久心息相依，丹田如常溫暖，此吾身有真鞴籥也。《道德經》云：「天地之間，其猶橐籥乎，虛而不屈，動而愈出」，是也。鼎者，乾也，性也。爐者，坤也，命也。既鼓動吾身之橐籥，必採藥物以入鼎。採藥之時，加武火之功，以性幹運於內，以命施化於外。片餉之間，乾坤合一，神炁交會，結成還丹，以為聖胎。故曰「真鼎爐」也。既得還丹成象，以文火溫養。虛心以守其性，實腹以養其命。恍惚杳冥之中，無中生有，有中生無，此即靜極復動，動極復靜。故曰「無中有，有中無」也。

14

托黃婆，媒姹女。輕輕地，默默舉。

黃婆、姹女，皆強名也。黃婆者，坤土也，即戊己土也，又言意也。姹女，兌金也。兌為少女，金隱水中。凡作丹，必托黃婆為媒，通姹女之情，以戊土藏火，火逼金行。當起火之初，受炁且柔，要當撥轉頂門關捩，從尾穴輕輕地、默默而舉。須臾火力熾盛，河車不可暫停。運入南宮，復還元位，嫁與金公而作老郎。崔公苦口叮嚀，以謂世人不達還丹之旨，故喻托以黃婆媒於姹女，直欲世人曉此理也。《悟真篇》云：「姹女遊行自有方，前行須短後須長，歸來卻入黃婆舍，嫁箇金公作老郎」，是也。

15

一日內，十二時，意所到，皆可為。

意者，性之用，即真土也。一日之內十二時辰，有一年之節候。自子時至辰巳六時屬陽，自午時至戌亥六時屬陰。一陽來復，身中子時也。一陰生姤，身中午時也。且夫水火間于南北，木金隔於東西，此四象何由而合？必假意以通消息，是以天地造化一刻可奪。一日之內十二時中，無晝無夜，念茲在茲。常惺惺地，動念以行火，息念以溫養火。此所以「意所到，皆可為」也。

16

飲刀圭，窺天巧。辨朔望，知昏曉。

飲者，宴也。刀者，水中金也。圭者，戊己真土也。言作丹採藥之時，必採水中之金，金不得自昇，必假戊土化火，逼逐金行，度上泥丸。金至此化為真液，如瓊漿甘露，一滴落於黃庭，宴之味之，津液甘美。故曰「飲刀圭」也。窺者，觀也。言能觀天道運化之功，遂執天而行，旋吾身斗柄之機，一刻之間能奪天地造化。故曰「窺天巧也」。《陰符經》所謂：「觀天之道，執天之行，盡矣」，純陽詩曰：「縱橫北斗心機巧，顛倒南辰膽氣雄」，是也。「辨朔望」者，以一歲言之，冬至為朔，夏至為

望；以一月言之，初一為朔，十五日為望；以一日言之，子時為
朔，午時為望；以一時言之，初一刻為朔，正四刻為望；以六十
四卦言之，復卦為朔，姤卦為望。以一身言之，尾穴為朔，泥丸
為望；子宮進火為朔，午位退符為望。既明此理，又要知其曉
昏。昏者，暮也。曉者，朝也。於卦有朝迍、暮蒙之理。一卦六
爻，顛倒用之，遂為兩卦。朝迍一陽生于下，暮蒙一陰生于上，
一陽一陰，一進一退，人身運化，與天地同也。達此理者，可以
長生久視，與鍾呂並駕，同日而語矣。有何疑哉！

17

識浮沉，明主客。要聚會，莫間隔。

浮者，汞也。沉者，鉛也。離汞居上曰浮，坎鉛居下曰沉。修丹
之訣，沉者必使其昇，浮者可使其降。故曰「識浮沉」也。既
「識浮沉」，須「明主客」。主者，命也。客者，性也。有身則
有命，有命則有性。性依命立，命從性修。是以命為性之母，故
為主；性為命之子，故為客。日逐之間，借身為用。仙師所謂
「讓他為主我為賓」，是也。既「明主客」，以鉛汞而同爐，主
客而同室，綿綿若存，於二六時中，迴光返照，打成一片，
（道）〔遍〕滿太虛。若夫時至氣化，機動籟鳴，火從臍下而
發，水向頂中而生，其妙自有不期然而然者。孔子所謂：「道也
者，不可須臾離也，可離，非道也」。程子亦云：「常心要在腔
子裏」。虛靖天師曰：「神一出便收來，神返身中炁自回，如此
朝朝與暮暮，自然赤子產靈胎」。此所以「要聚會，莫間隔」
也。

18

採藥時，調火功。受氣吉，防成凶。

「採藥時」者，乃身中一陽來復之時也。於斯時，則當閉關。行

火之功，妙在調燮停勻，從三關運轉，一舉三時，周流復位，萬氣凝真。當此之時，獨受於我神之暢快，喜慶難言。故曰「受炁吉」也。行火退符之間，務在存誠，一念不可間斷。設或纖毫差失，遂成凶矣。密意防護，不可不謹，是用野戰防危。故曰「防成凶」也。丹經云：「配合虎龍交姤處，此時如過小橋時」，是也。或曰：性靜無為，要坐便坐，要眠便眠。何必辨採藥調火？蓋不知有造化者耳，未足與議也。

19

火候足，莫傷丹。天地靈，造化慳。

鍊得黃芽滿鼎，白雪漫天，嬰兒成象，故「火候足」也。火候既足，只宜沐浴溫養。若不知止足，妄意行火，反傷丹矣。丹成之後，天地混合，神炁自靈，仙師所謂「虛室生白」，「神明自來」，故曰「天地靈」也。當此之時，宜加寶愛。調息務在微細，於靜定之中，內不出，外不入，形忘物忘，心同太虛，一炁純陽，故「造化慳」也。

20

初結胎，看本命。終脫胎，看四正。

祖劫天根，居混沌之中，乃為結胎之所。下手之初，鍊精化為炁，鍊氣化為神，鍊神化為虛，鍊虛合道，結為聖胎。初結胎之時，常於命蒂守之。故曰「初結胎，看本命」也。十月胎圓，移神上居泥丸，調神出殼。直待功成行滿，上帝詔臨。打破虛空，真人上舉，駕紅雲，跨白鶴，東西南北無所往而不可。故曰「終脫胎，看四正」。《靜中吟》云：「一朝功滿人不知，四面皆成夜光闕」，是也。

21

密密行，句句應。

此二句總結前八十句，言（大道金丹）〔金丹大道〕，進火退符，奪造化之妙訣。行之一身如空谷之應聲，陽燧之取火，方諸之取水。神通氣感，何其速之如是？故曰「密密行，句句應」。丹經云：「視之不見聽不聞，及至呼時又卻應」，是也。

掛金索

一更端坐，下手調元炁。混沌無言，絕念存真意。呼吸綿綿，配合居中位。撥轉些兒，黍米藏天地。

二更清淨，心要常虛守。默默回光，照見無中有。趕退群魔，振地金獅吼。頃刻功成，便與天齊壽。

三更雞叫，冬至陽初動。取坎填離，直向泥丸送。火運周天，爐內鉛投汞。九轉丹成，白雪飛仙洞。

四更安樂，萬事都無想。水滿華池，澆灌靈根長。靜裏乾坤，仙樂頻頻響。道大沖虛，名掛黃金榜。

五更月落，漸覺東方曉。谷裏真人，已見分明了。玉戶鸞驂，金頂龍蟠繞。打破虛空，萬道金光校。

GLOSSARY OF CHINESE CHARACTERS

For titles of texts not included in the present glossary, see the bibliography on p. 89.

"Aozhi" 奧旨 ("Concealed Teachings")
baixue 白雪 (White Snow)
Cantong qi 參同契 (The Seal of the Unity of the Three)
Chen Nan 陳楠 (?–1213)
Cheng Hao 程顥 (1032–85)
Cheng Yi 程頤 (1033–1107)
Chunyang 純陽 (Lü Dongbin)
chuqiao 出殼 ("exiting the shell")
Cui gong 崔公 (Master Cui)
Cui Xifan 崔希范 (ca. 880–940)
Cuixu pian 翠虛篇 (The Emerald Emptiness)
cuncheng 存誠 ("maintaining sincerity")
dadao jindan 大道金丹 (Golden Elixir of the Great Way)
dao 刀 ("blade, spatula, knife")
Daode jing 道德經 (Book of the Way and Its Virtue)
Daoxuan pian 道玄篇 (The Mystery of the Dao)
Daozang 道藏 (Taoist Canon)
Daozang jiyao 道藏輯要 (Essentials of the Taoist Canon)
Daxue 大學 (The Great Learning)
dizhi 地支 (earthly branches)
dongfang 洞房 (Cavern Chamber)
doubing 斗柄 (Dipper's Handle)
dumai 督脈 (Control vessel)
Duren jing 度人經 (Scripture on Salvation)
erwu 二物 ("two things")
fayan 法眼 ("Dharma-eye")
fangzhu 方諸 mirror

feng 風 ("wind")

fengguan 風關 (Barrier of Wind)

ganlu 甘露 (Sweet Dew)

geng 庚 (a celestial stem)

geng 更 ("vigil" of the night)

gui 癸 (a celestial stem)

haidi 海底 ("bottom of the sea")

hao 號 (appellation)

heche 河車 (River Chariot)

houtian 後天 ("postcelestial")

huachi 華池 (Flowery Pond)

Huandan fuming pian 還丹復命篇 (Returning to Life through the Reverted Elixir)

huandan 還丹 (Reverted Elixir)

huangdao 黃道 (the ecliptic)

huangfang 黃房 (Yellow Room)

Huangting jing 黃庭經 (Scripture of the Yellow Court)

huangya 黃芽 (Yellow Sprout)

Huanzhen ji 還真集 (Returning to Reality: A Collection)

Huanyuan pian 還元篇 (Returning to the Origin)

huiguang fanzhao 迴光返照 ("reversing the light and inverting the radiance")

Hun-Soul 魂

Hunran zi 渾然子

huohou 火候 (Fire Phases)

ji 己 (a celestial stem)

jia 甲 (a celestial stem)

jiaji 夾脊 (Spinal Handle)

jian 鑑 ("mirror")

jin 進 ("advancing")

jindan dadao 金丹大道 (Great Way of the Golden Elixir)

"Jindan shi" 金丹詩 ("Poem on the Golden Elixir")

Jindan sibai zi 金丹四百字 (Four Hundred Words on the Golden Elixir)

jing 鏡 ("mirror")

"Jingzhong yin" 靜中吟 ("Chant of Quiescence in the Center")

Jinhua zongzhi 金華宗旨 (Secret of the Golden Flower)

lao 老 ("old")

Li Daochun 李道純 (fl. 1288–92)

Li Panlong 李攀龍 (Ming dynasty)

Liaozhen zi 了真子 (Xiao Tingzhi)

Lingbao 靈寶 (Numinous Treasure)

Lü Dongbin 呂洞賓

luche 鹿車 ("deer chariot")

mihu 密戶 (Secret Door)

mimi 密密 ("closely")

ming 命 (Existence)

mingdi 命蒂 (Stem of Destiny; Stem of Life)

nangong 南宮 (Southern Palace)

Nanzong 南宗 (Southern Lineage)

Neidan 內丹 (Internal Alchemy)

nen 嫩 ("tender")

ni 逆 ("inverting the course")

niuche 牛車 ("ox chariot")

niwan 泥丸 (Muddy Pellet)

Peng Haogu 彭好古 (fl. 1599)

Po-Soul 魄

qi 氣 (Breath)

qian 慳 ("mean," "miserly, impoverished")

qiangming 強名 ("forced names")

qing 情 (emotions)

Qing'an Yingchan zi yulu 清庵瑩蟾子語錄 (Recorded Sayings of the Master Who Responds to the Cicadas in the Pure Retreat)

qiongjiang 瓊漿 (Jasper Wine)

Qingjing jing 清靜經 (Scripture of Clarity and Quiescence)

Qingjing miaojing zuantu jiezhu 清靜妙經纂圖解註 (Commentary on the Wondrous *Scripture of Clarity and Quiescence*, with Illustrations)

Qingtian ge 青天歌 (Song on the Azure Heaven)

Qingtian ge zhushi 青天歌註釋 (Explication of the Song on the Azure Heaven)

Qingxiu pai 清秀派 (Pure Cultivation branch [of Neidan])

Qiu Chuji 丘處機 (1148–1227)

Quanzhen 全真 (Complete Reality)

renmai 任脈 (Function vessel)

rentian yanmu 人天眼目 ("an eye for humans and deities")

ruyao 入藥 ("to enter the ingredients")

Ruyao jing 入藥鏡 (Mirror for Compounding the Medicine)

Ruyao jing zhujie 入藥鏡註解 (Commentary on the Mirror for Compounding the Medicine)

sanguan 三關 ("three barriers")

Santian yisui 三天易髓 (The Mutable Marrow of the Three Heavens)

shang 上 ("upper")

sheng 生 ("live")

shengmen 生門 (Gate of Life)

shengtai 聖胎 (Embryo of Sainthood)

Shi Jianwu 施肩吾 (fl. 820–35)

shi 時 ("hours"; time-units)

shun 順 ("following the course")

sixiang 四象 ("four images")

tiangang 天罡 (Celestial Net)

tiaoshen 調神 ("harmonizing the Spirit")

tufu 土釜 (Earthenware Crucible)

tui 退 ("withdrawing")

waidan 外丹 (External Elixir; External Alchemy)

Wang Daoyuan 王道淵 (Wang Jie)

Wang Jie 王玠 (?–ca. 1380)

Wang Zihua 汪子華 (714–89)

weilü 尾閭 (Caudal Funnel)

weixue 尾穴 (Caudal Cavity)

"Wenyan" 文言 ("Explanation of the Sentences")

wu 戊 (a celestial stem)

Wuzhen pian 悟真篇 (Awakening to Reality)

xia 下 ("lower")

xiang 象 ("image")

xiantian 先天 ("precelestial")

Xiao Tingzhi 蕭廷芝 (fl. 1260–64)

xiaoxi 消息 ("ebb and flow")

Xiaozai huming miaojing 消灾護命妙經 (Wondrous Scripture on Averting Disaster and Protecting Life)

Xiaozai huming miaojing zhu 消灾護命妙經註 (Commentary on the *Wondrous Scripture on Averting Disaster and Protecting Life*)

"Xici" 繫辭 ("Appended Sayings")

xing 形 ("form")

xing 性 (Nature)

xinggeng 性根 (Root of Nature)

Xiujiang 修江 (Jiangxi Province)

Xiushui 修水 (Jiangxi Province)

xuanguan yiqiao 玄關一竅 (Mysterious Barrier)

Xue Daoguang 薛道光 (1078?–1191)

yanghuo 陽火 (Yang Fire)

yangsui 陽燧 mirror

yezhan 野戰 ("fight in the wild")

yi 意 (Intention)

Yijing 易經 (Book of Changes)

yike 一刻 ("a while"; ca. 15 minutes)

yinfu 陰符 (Yin Response)

Yinfu jing 陰符經 (Scripture of the Hidden Agreement)

Yinfu jing jiasong jiezhu 陰符經夾頌解註 (Commentary on the *Scripture of the Hidden Agreement*)

yinian 一念 ("one instant," "one thought")

Yinyang pai **陰陽派** (Yin-Yang branch [of Neidan])

Yu Yan 俞琰 (1258–1314)

Yunfang 雲房 (Zhongli Quan)

yuzhen 玉枕 (Jade Pillow)

Zhang Boduan 張伯端 (987?–1082)

Zhang Jixian 張繼先 (1092–1126)

Zhang Wumeng 張無夢 (952–1051)

Zhang Yuchu 張宇初 (1361–1410)

Zhang Ziyang 張紫陽 (Zhang Boduan)

"Zhaohun" 招魂 ("Summoning the Hun-Soul")

zhengqi 正氣 (correct Breaths)

zhenren 真人 (True Man)

zhi 質 ("matter," "concrete substance")

zhizhi 知止 ("knowing when to stop")
zhizu 知足 ("knowing what is sufficient")
Zhong-Lü 鐘呂
Zhonghe ji 中和集 (Anthology of Central Harmony)
Zhongli Quan 鍾離權
Zhongpai 中派 (Central Branch [of Neidan])
Zhongyong 中庸 (The Doctrine of the Mean)
Zhuangzi 莊子
zi 子 (earthly branch; name of a "double hour")
Ziyang 紫陽 (Zhang Boduan)

WORKS QUOTED

Chinese Texts

Cantong qi 參同契 [The Seal of the Unity of the Three]. Attr. Wei Boyang 魏伯陽 (trad. second century). Text in Fabrizio Pregadio, *The Seal of the Unity of the Three* (see below, "Western-Language Works").

Chuci 楚辭 [Songs of Chu]. Fourth to first centuries BCE. Sibu beiyao 四部備要 ed.

Cuixu pian 翠虛篇 [The Emerald Emptiness]. Chen Nan 陳楠 (?–1213). Daozang 道藏 ed., CT 1090.

Daode jing 道德經 [Book of the Way and its Virtue]. Fourth to third centuries BCE (?). Ed. by Zhu Qianzhi 朱謙之, *Laozi jiaoshi* 老子校釋 (Beijing: Zhonghua shuju, 1984).

Daofa huiyuan 道法會元 [A Collection of Sources of Taoist Methods]. Ca. 1400. Daozang 道藏 ed., CT 1220.

Daoshu 道樞 [Pivot of the Dao]. Zeng Zao 曾慥, ca. 1150. Daozang 道藏 ed., CT 1017.

Daxue 大學 [The Great Learning]. Prob. third century BCE. Text in James Legge, *Confucian Analects, The Great Learning, and The Doctrine of the Mean* (see below, "Western-Language Works").

Er Cheng yishu 二程遺書 [Writings Bequeathed by the Cheng Brothers]. Cheng Yi 程頤 (1033–1107) and Cheng Hao 程顥 (1032–85). Sibu beiyao 四部備要 ed.

Huandan fuming pian 還丹復命篇 [Returning to Life through the Reverted Elixir]. Xue Daoguang 薛道光 (1078?–1191). Daozang 道藏 ed., CT 1088.

Huangting neijing jing 黃庭內景經 [Scripture of the Inner Effulgences of the Yellow Court]. Late fourth century. In *Yunji qiqian* 雲笈七籤 [Seven Lots from the Bookcase of the Clouds], Daozang 道藏 ed., CT 1032, 11–12.27b.

Huangting waijing jing 黃庭外景經 [Scripture of the Outer Effulgences of the Yellow Court]. Second or third century century. In *Yunji qiqian* 雲笈七籤 [Seven Lots from the Bookcase of the Clouds], Daozang 道藏 ed., CT 1032, 12.28a–56b.

Huanzhen ji 還真集 [Returning to Reality]. Wang Jie 王玠 (?–ca. 1380). Daozang 道藏 ed., CT 1074.

Jindan da chengji 金丹大成集 [A Great Anthology on the Golden Elixir]. Xiao Tingzhi 蕭廷芝 (fl. 1260–64). In *Xiuzhen shishu* 修真十書 [Ten Books on the Cultivation of Reality; ca. 1300], ch. 9–13. Daozang 道藏 ed., CT 263.

Jindan wenda 金丹問答 [Questions and Answers on the Golden Elixir]. Xiao Tingzhi 蕭廷芝 (fl. 1260–64). In *Xiuzhen shishu* 修真十書 [Ten Books on the Cultivation of Reality; ca. 1300], ch. 10. Daozang 道藏 ed., CT 263.

Jinlian zhengzong ji 金蓮正宗記 [Records of the Correct Lineage of the Golden Lotus]. Qin Zhi'an 秦志安 (1188–1244). Daozang 道藏 ed., CT 173.

Lingbao wuliang duren shangpin miaojing 靈寶無量度人上品妙經 [Wondrous Scripture of the Upper Chapters of the Numinous Treasure on Limitless Salvation]. Original text, ca. 400; commentary, twelfth century. Daozang 道藏 ed., CT 1.

Sanshi dai tianshi Xujing zhenjun yulu 三十代天師虛靖真君語錄 [Recorded Sayings of the Thirtieth Generation Celestial Master, True Lord of Empty Quiescence]. Ed. by Zhang Yuchu 張宇初 (1361–1410). Daozang 道藏 ed., CT 1249.

Wuzhen pian 悟真篇 [Awakening to Reality]. Zhang Boduan 張伯端 (987?–1082). Text in Wang Mu 王沐, *Wuzhen pian qianjie (wai san zhong)* 『悟真篇』淺解（外三種）[A simple explanation of the *Wuzhen pian* and three other works] (Beijing: Zhonghua shuju, 1990).

Yijing 易經 [Book of Changes]. Original portions ca. ninth century BCE, commentaries and appendixes ca. 350 to 250 BCE. Text in *Zhouyi yinde* 周易引得 (A Concordance to Yi Ching). Peking: Harvard-Yenching Institute, 1935.

Yinfu jing 陰符經 [Scripture of the Hidden Agreement]. Ca. 600 (?). Text in *Huangdi yinfu jing zhu* 黃帝陰符經註 (Commentary to the Yellow Emperor's Scripture of the Hidden Agreement), with commentary by Yu Yan 俞琰 (1258–1314). Daozang 道藏 ed., CT 125.

Zhonghe ji [Anthology of Central Harmony]. Li Daochun 李道純 (fl. 1288–92). Daozang 道藏 ed., CT 249.

Zhongyong 中和集 [The Doctrine of the Mean]. Prob. third/second century BCE. Text in James Legge, *Confucian Analects, The Great Learning, and The Doctrine of the Mean* (see below, "Western-Language Works").

Zhouyi cantong qi fahui 周易參同契發揮 [Elucidation of the *Cantong qi*]. Yu Yan 俞琰, 1284. Daozang 道藏 ed., CT 1005.

Zhuangzi 莊子 [Book of Master Zhuang Zhou]. Original portions fourth century BCE, completed in the second century BCE. Ed. by Guo Qingfan 郭慶藩, *Zhuangzi jishi* 莊子集釋 (Beijing: Zhonghua shuju, 1961).

Western-Language Works

Bokenkamp, Stephen. *Early Daoist Scriptures*. Berkeley: University of California Press, 1997.

Cleary, Thomas. *Understanding Reality: A Taoist Alchemical Classic*. Honolulu: University of Hawaii Press, 1987.

Legge, James. *Confucian Analects, The Great Learning, and The Doctrine of the Mean*. Second revised edition. Oxford: Clarendon Press, 1893. [*The Chinese Classics*, vol. 1.]

Pregadio, Fabrizio. *Awakening to Reality: The "Regulated Verses" of the* Wuzhen pian, *a Taoist Classic of Internal Alchemy*. Mountain View: Golden Elixir Press, 2009.

Pregadio, Fabrizio. *The Seal of the Unity of the Three: A Study and Translation of the* Cantong qi, *the Source of the Taoist Way of the Golden Elixir*. Mountain View, Golden Elixir Press, 2011.

Wang Mu. *Foundations of Internal Alchemy: The Taoist Practice of Neidan*. Mountain View, Ca: Golden Elixir Press, 2011.

Watson, Burton. *The Complete Works of Chuang Tzu*. New York: Columbia University Press, 1968.

Wilhelm, Richard. *The I Ching or Book of Changes*. New York: Bollingen, 1950.

Golden Elixir Press

www.goldenelixir.com
press@goldenelixir.com

Golden Elixir Press publishes dependable and affordable books on Taoism, Taoist alchemy, and other traditional doctrines, in print and as e-books

Wang Jie, *Commentary on the Mirror for Compounding the Medicine: A Fourteenth-Century Work on Taoist Internal Alchemy*. 2013.

Fabrizio Pregadio, *The Seal of the Unity of the Three*. Vol. 2. *Bibliographic Studies on the* Cantong qi: *Commentaries, Essays, and Related Texts*. 2012.

Fabrizio Pregadio, *The Seal of the Unity of the Three: A Study and Translation of the* Cantong qi, *the Source of the Taoist Way of the Golden Elixir*. 2011.

Isabelle Robinet, *The World Upside Down: Essays on Taoist Internal Alchemy*. 2011.

Wang Mu, *Foundations of Internal Alchemy: The Taoist Practice of Neidan*. 2011.

Ananda K. Coomaraswamy, *Hinduism and Buddhism*. 2011.

Jami, *Flashes of Light: A Treatise on Sufism*. 2010.

Shaikh Sharfuddin Maneri, *Letters from a Sufi Teacher*. 2010.

Fabrizio Pregadio, *Awakening to Reality: The "Regulated Verses" of the* Wuzhen pian, *a Taoist Classic of Internal Alchemy*. 2009.

Fabrizio Pregadio, *Chinese Alchemy: An Annotated Bibliography of Works in Western Languages*. 2009.

Fabrizio Pregadio, *Index of Zhonghua Daozang*. 2009.

CPSIA information can be obtained at www.ICGtesting.com
Printed in the USA
LVOW13s2003131113

361176LV00001B/131/P